The Pubs of Ludlow and Neighbouring Villages

GW00578689

The Pubs of Ludlow and Neighbouring Villages

by

Tony Hobbs

Logaston Press

LOGASTON PRESS
Little Logaston Woonton Almeley
Herefordshire HR3 6QH

First published by Logaston Press 2002
Copyright © Tony Hobbs 2002

ISBN 1 873827 83 0

Set in Times by Logaston Press
and printed in Great Britain by
Bell and Bain Ltd., Glasgow.

This book is dedicated to my sisters,
Gillian and Jenny,
for their forbearance and understanding.

Contents

Sources of Illustrations

Shropshire County Museum Service, Ludlow Museum collection
pp. 30 (upper), 42, 86, 98, 108, 132, 141, 168 (upper), 170, 175

Shropshire Records and Research Centre
p. 58

Herefordshire Libraries (Leominster)
pp. 60, 99

Harvey Griffiths
pp. 37 (upper & lower), 43, 54 (upper and lower), 69, 71, 75, 94, 100, 125

Alf Jenkins
pp. 191 (top right), 192 (upper and lower), 195

Ron Shoesmith
pp. 23, 24 (upper, plan), 25 (right), 26, 32, 33, 38 (lower), 40, 41, 45, 47, 48, 50, 53, 60 (lower), 61 (lower), 65 (upper & lower), 74, 76 (lower), 77, 79 (upper), 80, 87, 89, 102, 107, 109, 113, 116, 120, 123, 126, 133, 137, 139, 143, 145 (lower), 165 (top & bottom), 166, 170 (lower), 171, 172

Charlton Arms
p. 78 (upper & lower)

Golden Lion, Knowle
pp. 197, 198 (upper & lower)

Brettons of Ludlow
pp. 31, 39, 150, 152, 162

Halls Ltd.
pp. 188 (lower), 189 (upper), 190

John Norton
pp. 56, 96, 125, 129, 161,

Donald Burmingham
p. 30 (lower)

Graham Willson-Lloyd
p. 90

David Faulkner
p. 168

Peter Klein
p. 169

David Williams (deceased)
p. 152

Tony Brooks
p. 177

Clifford Smout
p. 180

Gillian Simonds
p. 103

Acknowledgments

In putting together this volume, the first in this series to cover inns and taverns in Shropshire, I have been following in the footsteps of three men, to whom I owe a debt of gratitude.

Firstly, my thanks go to Ron Shoesmith, who wrote *The Pubs of Hereford City*, the first title to be published in this 'Pubs of ...' series. He was always on hand to lend advice and encouragement and was responsible for many of the illustrations, both photographs and line drawings.

Secondly, my thanks go to the late Harry Baker who brought out the *Alphabet of Ludlow Pubs* in 1983, which contains a wealth of information. Harry was a reporter on the *Ludlow Advertiser*, before going on to the *Birmingham Mail*, and had a family connection at the Smithfield pub in Lower Galdeford.

I am also grateful to local historian Edmund Jones, who wrote the *Old Inns of Ludlow* in 1913, which includes information dating to the 16th century and a list of inns, by wards, for the year 1792.

My main areas of research were the Ludlow Museum (where Howard and Daniel were particularly helpful); the Ludlow Library (where Jenny was a mine of information); the Shropshire Records and Research Centre in Shrewsbury; the Leominster Library; and the Herefordshire Record Office. At the Museum, I came across the printing records and personal diaries of Mr. T. Griffiths, a Ludlow printer in the 19th century, which were of great interest.

Important contributions were made by Tony Banks, former land-lord of the Blue Boar, who lent me the 1931 to 1961 minutes for the Ludlow and District Licensed Victuallers' Association; Harvey Griffiths, for kindly allowing me to reproduce a number of old post-cards from his collection; and Alf Jenkins, who gave permission to use quotes and photographs about the Dhustone Inn from his book, *Titterstone Clee Hills*.

Finally, my thanks go to all the landlords for their help and to the present owners of pubs which have become private residences, namely: Royal Oak, Culmington; New Inn, Stanton Lacy; Serpent, Ashford Carbonel; Dhustone, Clee Hill; and Crown, Knowbury.

The sources of many of the illustrations used in this book are listed separately. The rest are from the author's own collection.

Tony Hobbs
September 2002

'Here's to all friends around the Wrekin'.

(Traditional Shropshire toast)

Introduction

With four volumes already written about the inns and taverns of Herefordshire, it was perhaps only logical that the next step should be into Shropshire, a county renowned for its brew pubs and fine foods. Where better to start than Ludlow, generally regarded as the provincial 'gourmet capital', and home to some of the finest hostelries that have existed.

As my publisher pointed out, it would be a labour of love to write about the inns of Ludlow, which, indeed, it was. So steeped in ancient matters is the town that it was almost like a re-enactment of an English history book. And, of course, once you start delving into a particular building's past or a certain aspect of local history, you become ensnared. Then it becomes a question of where to draw the line, where to stop. But, like most things, writing a book is governed by time and there was never enough of this before the publishing date loomed.

So, although this book cannot do full justice to the complexity of the vast number of buildings which have at some time or other sold beer or liquor, I feel it gives a lively insight into the life and times of Ludlow inns and taverns. As an appetizer, the book gives a basic history of the inn, how it has changed over the ages, and the changes that have taken place in the licensing laws, followed by details of the growth of brewing and breweries and of that essential product beer, or ale, particularly real ale.

The ensuing chapters cover Ludlow area by area with a pub-by-pub description which, with the aid of the street maps, the reader should be able to recognise. I say this because the majority, including several large hotels, have closed and few identification marks remain. Where appropriate, there is a description of some local practice or custom such as bull-baiting in the Bull Ring, a tug-of-war competition in Castle Square, circuses in Old Street, and, in Tower Street, near the prison, a reminder of some of the dreadful punishments that were meted out for misdemeanours and felonies.

Of necessity, some of the inns were built in the suburbs of Ludlow—these are covered in the penultimate chapter—but then the danger arose how far out of town did one go. Having already travelled some way along the A4117, it was decided to stop at Clee Hill, a remarkable village having strong links with Ludlow.

As with the other volumes in this series, it is suspected that this book may prompt many memories, which you may care to share and which may lead eventually to an up-date of this title.

Tony Hobbs
September 2002

> The troubles of our proud and angry dust
> Are from eternity, and shall not fail.
> Bear them we can, and if we can we must.
> Shoulder the sky, my lad, and drink your ale.
>
> (A.E. Housman, *Last Poems*, 1922)

CHAPTER ONE

Alehouses, Taverns and Inns

O I have been to Ludlow fair
And left my necktie God knows where,
And carried half way home, or near,
Pints and quarts of Ludlow beer:
Then the world seemed none so bad,
And I myself a sterling lad;
And down in lovely muck I've lain,
Happy till I woke again.

(*A Shropshire Lad*, A.E. Housman, 1896)

The alcoholic drinking place, or inn, was probably introduced into this country when the first roads were formally laid out by the Romans. During their 400-year occupation of Britain, the Romans built something like 10,000 miles of road. Initially the roads linked places of military importance and broke up enemy territory, but eventually they formed a national network for all travellers. As G.K. Chesterton observed: 'Before the Roman came to Rye or out to Severn strode, The rolling English drunkard made the rolling English road'. In Shropshire, the main routes were from Wroxeter, the fourth largest town in England, towards London and between the legionary fortresses of Chester in the north and Caerleon in south Wales. The Chester road passed through Wroxeter and then went close to present day Craven Arms and onto the Roman forts at Leintwardine and Kenchester, in Herefordshire, before reaching Caerleon.

Alcoholic refreshment, mainly in the form of wine but also cider and ale, would have been served along these and other routes. There were usually *mansiones* and *diversoria* along the roads and *tabernae* in the towns. One of the commonest signs was a Chequer Board—of

1

Roman origin having been found on houses in Pompeii, and referring to a game such as chess or draughts. A bush of vine leaves, symbolical of Bacchus, the god of wine, was often displayed above the door of *tabernae*.

After the departure of the Romans in the early 5th century, the country descended into the Dark Ages. There are no traces of Saxon ale houses, built of wood and wattle and daub, but it is certain that inns were a feature of English life in 600 AD for there exist decrees of Ethelbert, King of Kent, in 616, and of Ina, King of Wessex, in 730, for regulating the number of ale sellers and for keeping the inns in better order. By 750 the Archbishop of York issued a Canon 'That no priest go to eat or drink in taverns', and there were so many inns by the time of King Edgar (959-75) that he issued a decree limiting their number to one per village.

In those times ale houses were indistinguishable from other domestic dwellings, and while customers, some clerical, drank indoors, off sales business was also conducted. Much brewing was done on a communal basis, as with the church ales. These were specially brewed ales sold to the public with the money raised going for church purposes.

Immediately after the Norman Conquest the country was parcelled out amongst the newcomers and, with warfare still raging along the Welsh border, numerous castles were built. The castles in turn generated settlements outside their walls. One such castle was at Ludlow followed by a new town laid out in a grid pattern by the 12th century. During this century the Marcher lordships emerged as buffer states, almost indeed as independent fiefdoms, between the Welsh and English royal authority. A century later Ludlow was one of just over 100 towns in England and Wales to be fortified with a full circuit of walls.

These new towns with growing populations inevitably resulted in a sizeable increase in the number of inns and taverns. However, permanent alehouses only start to appear in significant numbers in the 13th century.

Various measures to protect the customer were introduced including the 'Assize of Bread and Ale' in 1267. This enactment accepted the principle that both bread and ale were necessities of life and, for a period of some 300 years, it ensured that the retail price of ale was fixed according to the prices of corn and malt. At that time, ale was usually made from malted barley, or occasionally wheat, which was steeped in water and then fermented with yeast.

During the 13th century there was a gradual increase in the sale of wine, and a separation came into being between 'taverns' which sold both ale and wine, and 'alehouses' which sold only ale. In addition to these there were the wayside inns or 'hostels' that provided accommodation for pilgrims and other travellers as well as food and drink.

Outside the towns, the principal hospitality for travellers during the medieval period was provided by monasteries. The great monastic houses, especially those situated along the main roads, were the halting places for all who travelled. During the 14th and 15th centuries, a gradual change occurred as merchants began to travel and the influence of the church began to wane.

By the late Middle Ages ale was the only safe liquid to drink and people drank it all day. For breakfast 'small beer', a weaker beer made from a second boiling of the barley mash, and at other times strong ale. There was no alternative until tea was introduced at the end of 18th century. After 1,000 years of ale drinking an important change occurred in the early 15th century with the introduction of hops and the resultant manufacture of beer. Although described by the authorities in Shrewsbury as that 'wicked and pernicious weed' the hop not only gave extra flavour but contained preservative properties enabling the beverage to be kept much longer than ale before 'going-off'.

An evergreen bush indicating an inn, from a 14th-century manuscript.

The first formal licensing law at the end of the 15th century empowered Justices of the Peace to obtain sureties for good behaviour from landlords and, if necessary, to close alehouses. Some 50 years later the Justices obtained the power, which they still retain, to both licence and

A 14th century inn, from a 14th-century psalter.

suppress alehouses—hence 'licensed premises'. Legislation continued, and 1553 saw an Act of Parliament curtailing the number of 'taverns', with most towns restricted to one, and thereby limiting the sale of wine. But there were still plenty of alehouses in which to drink with about 44 alehouses for every tavern in the latter part of the 16th century. This was equivalent to more than one drinking establishment for every 200 persons, a far higher ratio than exists today.

Ludlow grew rich trading in wool and cloth, and the 1377 poll tax returns showed that the town ranked as the 34th largest in England with a population of 1,700. The new parish church of St. Laurence, one of the most beautiful churches in England, contains a remarkable series of 28 misericords in the choir stalls, carved in the 15th century and illustrating medieval town life. One misericord shows a drunken tapster, sometimes called 'Simon the Cellarer', in late 14th century costume and drawing ale or wine from a barrel. Pots, jugs and barrels are shown in detail. It may be a truthful representation as many taverns of 15th-century Ludlow were in cellars, or it may represent a servant who is abusing his trust.

During the 14th and 15th centuries the borderland was dominated by the great Marcher families

'Simon the Cellarer' on a misericord in Ludlow parish church.

4

and in particular by the Mortimers, including Roger (IV) who plotted the overthrow of Edward II and entertained his Queen at Ludlow Castle. In the 1450s Ludlow was the base of Richard, duke of York, son of Anne Mortimer, who challenged the rule of Henry VI in the Wars of the Roses. In 1459 the Yorkist forces melted away overnight in the face of overwhelming Lancastrian might with the king at its head at the nominal battle of Ludford Bridge, after which Ludlow was pillaged. A year later the duke was killed in the Battle of Wakefield. However, his son Edward, earl of March, defeated the Lancastrians at Mortimers Cross, near Ludlow, in 1461 and was subsequently proclaimed King Edward IV on his arrival in London. The same year he granted a special charter to Ludlow for 'laudable and gratuitous services'.

Ludlow now became a royal castle, to which the king sent his sons Edward and Richard, and in 1475 the Council in the Marches was set up to govern Wales and the Borders on behalf of the infant Prince of Wales, with Ludlow chosen as its headquarters. Later, Henry VII sent Arthur to rule Wales from Ludlow and in the next reign Princess Mary was despatched to Ludlow with a council which was both a household and a court.

The next 200 years were halcyon times for Ludlow, which was the capital not only of the Marches but virtually of the whole of Wales. The Council performed important functions in criminal, civil and ecclesiastical law. The President resided in the castle while some of the judges and many attorneys, pursuivants and clerks lived in the town. As Edward Jones wrote in *Old Inns of Ludlow*, 'The jurisdiction of the Court of the Marches brought large numbers of strangers into the town from long distances, and the demand for lodging and victualling accommodation would, as a natural consequence, develop the extension of inns in the town'. Those engaged in these services accounted for nearly a fifth of all tradespeople in Ludlow in the early 1600s.

By 1626 recognisances to sell beer or ale were granted to over 100 Ludlow residents, but only 16 of these had inns known by their signs. These were: **Anchor**, 28-30 Broad Street; **Angel**, 9 Broad Street; **Antyloppe**, 49 Broad Street; **Bell**, 21 Bell Lane; **Bull**, 14 Bull Ring; **Cross Keys**, (Church Inn); **Crown**, 56-58 Broad Street; **Falcon**, 52 Broad Street; **George**, 8 High Street; **Green Dragon**, 9 Corve Street;

16  **99**

Whereas by the Laws and Statutes of This Realm

NOTICE

IS HEREBY GIVEN TO ALL

INN KEEPERS, ALEHOUSE KEEPERS, SUTLERS, VICTUALLERS

and other Retailers of

ALE and BEER

AND EVERY OTHER PERSON or PERSONS KEEPING A PUBLIC HOUSE
IN ANY
CITY, TOWN CORPORATE, BOROUGH, MARKET TOWN, VILLAGE, HAMLET, PARISH,
PART or PLACE IN THE *Kingdom of England*

That, as from the **24th** *day of* JUNE. **1700**

THEY SHALL BE REQUIRED TO RETAIL and SELL THEIR ALE & BEER

by the FULL ALE QUART or PINT

According to the Laid Standard

IN VESSELS DULY MARKED with W.R and CROWN

be they made of

WOOD. GLASS, HORN, LEATHER or PEWTER etc.

Any Person Retailing Ale or Beer to a **TRAVELLER** *or* **WAYFARER** *in Vessels not signed and marked as aforesaid will be liable to a* **PENALTY** *not exceeding*

FORTY SHILLINGS

FOR EVERY SUCH OFFENCE

By Act of Parliament ~ at WESTMINSTER
In the Reign of Our Sovereign ~ WILLIAM III by the Grace of God, King,
Defender of the Faith &c

Gryffyn, 23 Bull Ring; **Harp**, 102 Corve Street; **Red Lyon**, 3 Old Street/13 Tower Street; **Rose & Crown**, 145 Corve Street; **Star**, 24-25 Broad Street; and the **Talbot**, 139 Corve Street.

Although Ludlow became the social centre for the gentry of South Shropshire and North Herefordshire in the 17th century everything was not always rosy. The sewerage consisted of open drains running down the streets and undesirable characters were much in evidence. This led to a levy in 1630 to 'maintain the beedles to keep rogues and sturdy vagbonds out of the town'.

During the Civil War, Ludlow was the last significant Royalist stronghold to survive in Shropshire, before being captured by Cromwell's forces in 1645. The Council in the Marches had continued to exercise authority under James I and Charles I, but was suspended during the Interregnum, and after a revival under Charles II was finally dissolved in 1689. It is interesting to note that during the Commonwealth period in Shropshire only Parliamentarians were allowed to hold licences. After the Restoration the old ale-stake (the pole projecting from the front of an inn) outside licensed premises was replaced by the painted inn sign.

With the arrival of William of Orange, a Dutchman, to the throne in 1689, the distillation of gin, a Dutch drink, was encouraged. Exempt from duty it was also much cheaper than ale and soon it was being sold from every small alehouse. Until well into the 18th century there was what Monkton in his *History of the English Public House* described as 'one of the biggest orgies of over-indulgence our island history has ever seen'. The result was that consumption of spirits increased from half a million gallons in 1684 to over nine million gallons in 1758. While beer and ale were foods and part of the nation's diet, gin was a poison as Hogarth's famous prints of the horrors of 'Gin Lane' and the prosperous 'Beer Street' illustrated. The various 'Gin Acts' that followed, together with increased duties and a strengthening of the powers of the justices, rapidly changed this trend and by 1758 excise duty was paid on less than two million gallons per year. The 'gin era' was over.

Means of regulating public houses continued to attract government interest, however, and from 1729 licences had to be renewed annually at Brewster Sessions.

The end of the 17th century saw the beginning of the new coaching era and with it the golden age of the inn, providing food and accommodation for travellers.

> Whoe'er has travelled life's dull round,
> Where'er his stages may have been
> May sigh to think how oft he found
> The warmest welcome - at an inn.
>
> (Shenstone, poet—*Written at an Inn*, 18th century)

Boswell, in his *Life of Samuel Johnson,* painted a cheerful picture:

There is no private house in which people can enjoy themselves so well as at a capital tavern ... The master of the house is anxious to entertain his guests; the guests are anxious to be agreeable to him; and no man but a very imprudent dog indeed can as freely command what is in another man's house as if it were his own. Whereas, at a tavern, there is a general freedom from anxiety. You are sure you are welcome; and the more noise you make, the more trouble you give, the more good things you call for, the welcomer you are. No servants will attend you with the alacrity which waiters do, who are incited by the prospect of an immediate reward in proportion as they please. No, sir, there is nothing which has yet been contrived by man, by which so much happiness is produced, as by a good tavern or inn.

And Boswell heard the great doctor assert that 'a tavern chair was the throne of human felicity'.

In contrast, the fifth Viscount Torrington, who, as the Hon. John Byng, covered thousands of English miles and sampled the fare of hundreds of English inns between 1781 and 1794, had this to say:

The imposition in travelling is abominable; the innkeepers are insolent, the hostlers are sulky, the chambermaids are pert, and the waiters are impertinent; the meat is tough, the wine is foul, the beer is hard, the sheets are wet, the linnen is dirty, and the knives are never clean'd!! Every home is better than this?

However, it is a testimony to the fineness of his discrimination that he commended Ludlow as the loveliest town in all England!

The early 19th century was the culmination of coach travel and inns were then at the height of their prosperity. In *Going on a Journey*, the essayist and critic William Hazlitt had this to say:

How fine it is to enter some old town, walled and turreted just at the approach of night-fall, or to come to some straggling village, with the lights streaming through the surrounding gloom; and then after inquiring for the best entertainment that the place affords, to 'take one's ease at one's inn!' These eventful moments in our lives' history are too precious, too full of solid, heart-felt happiness to be frittered and dribbled away in imperfect sympathy. I would have them all to myself, and drain them to the last drop: they will do to talk of or to write about afterwards ... The *incognito* of an inn is one of its striking privileges — 'lord of one's-self, uncumber'd with a name'. Oh! it is great to shake off the trammels of the world and of public opinion ... to be known by no other title but *the Gentleman in the parlour*.

Ludlow boasted many 'commodious inns' which 'possess[ed] superior accommodation', including the **Crown**, the **Angel** and the **Feathers**, the latter arguably one of the finest inn buildings in the whole country. They provided refreshment for travellers, local people and for the crowds at markets and fairs. At the end of the 17th century there were no fewer than 173 stables at inns in the town.

By 1745 there were 49 inns and alehouses in Ludlow, a number which increased to 55 in 1792, distributed over the town as follows: 16 in Castle Street ward; eight in Broad Street ward; 23 in Old Street and Galdeford ward; and eight in Corve Street ward. In 1790 the *Universal British Directory* described Ludlow thus: 'It is a very clean, well-built place and is the residence of many people of rank and fortune'. Every kind of function was held at the inns ranging from auctions and political gatherings to entertainments including cock-fighting and prize-fighting. Even so, by 1822 the number had dropped to 46, plus an additional dozen beer retailers.

With Ludlow being a 'market town - since time out of mind', country people walked or rode into market, many of them by the carriers' carts which operated regularly to and from surrounding towns and villages, usually terminating at Ludlow pubs. In 1885 there were 47 departures a week, including 13 from the **George**, nine from the **Globe**, eight from the **Portcullis**, and seven from the **Compasses**.

The lads in their hundred to Ludlow
come in for the fair,
There's men from the barn and the forge
and the mill and the fold,
The lads for the girls and the lads
for the liquor are there,
And there with the rest are the lads
that will never be old.

(*A Shropshire Lad*, A.E. Houseman)

Modes of travelling were changing with the 'iron horse' making vast strides all over the country and reaching Ludlow in 1852, and by 1860 stagecoach travelling had come to an end in the town. This had an affect on the town's hostelries with a number closing down, despite a 30% increase in population (from 3,897 in 1801 to 5,087 in 1871).

It was during the 19th century that most of the legislation that affects the present-day consumption and sale of alcoholic drink was enacted. The Alehouse Act of 1828 meant that the licensee no longer had to find sureties for his behaviour. However, he was bound to use the legal, stamped measures, not to adulterate his drinks, and not to permit drunkenness on his premises. The Beerhouse Acts of 1830, 1834 and 1840 followed, resulting in a proliferation of beer-houses, many in country areas. At that time there were few restrictions on licensing hours. As a whole, the only non-permitted hours were during Divine Services on Sundays, Christmas Day and Good Friday. At the beginning of the 20th century public houses were, in general, still allowed to open for some 20 hours each day.

The turn of the 19th century witnessed another population increase with the construction of the great pipeline to carry drinking water from the Elan Valley reservoirs to Birmingham which passed through Ludlow. A large number of people in the town were employed on that work. While good for trade, drunkenness increased with drunken navvies from 'the pipe track' found every day lying on the seats of Castle Walk and under the walls of the castle. This was no doubt one of the reasons why the Ludlow magistrates seemed bent on reducing further the number of licensed premises. Even the solicitor to the Ludlow and District Victuallers' Association admitted that 'there may be too many licences in some parts of the town'. The *Ludlow Advertiser* called on the Victuallers' Association and the magistrates to agree some kind of planned reduction in licences, as had successfully been done in Birmingham, where, between 1904 and 1914, 1,000 licences disappeared.

The police chief, Supt. James Perry, reported at the annual licensing sessions for the borough of Ludlow in February 1911, that there were 39 public houses and one beerhouse for a population of 6,328 (based on the 1901 census). This worked out at one license to about every 158 persons. One licensed person was proceeded against and convicted during the year; 'with that exception the other houses have been fairly well conducted'. With reference to offences against the Licensing Act the following number had been proceeded against during the past three years: 1908, 86; 1909, 59; 1910, 59 (of the latter number 21 were against non-residents).

The 'borough' referred to the immediate town, whilst 'county' referred to the surrounding district. Thus, in the same period Ludlow (County) Licensing Session reported there were 21 public houses and two beer houses to a population of 9,634 (1901 census). This showed one licensed house to almost every 419 of the population. With reference to offences against the Licensing Act the following number were proceeded against during the past thee years: 1908, 45; 1909, 46; 1910, 43.

It is not often realised that the regulations concerning licensed houses, alcohol and children are mainly of 20th century origin. Although the 1872 Act made it an offence to sell spirits to those using licensed premises under the age of 16, it was not until the Children's Act of 1908 that children under the age of 14 were prohibited in licensed premises. It was only in 1923 that it became, in general, an offence to serve alcoholic drinks to those under 18.

The First World War brought about more drinking restrictions. In November 1915, Colonel A.H.J. Doyle, commanding the 53rd Area, Western Command, issued an Order under the Defence of the Realm Act to all licensees in Shropshire curtailing the hours for the opening of licensed premises. They were allowed to open on week days only between the hours of 10.30 a.m. and 9 p.m., and on Sundays between 12.30 and 2.30 p.m. and 6.30 to 9 p.m. This led to the Ludlow and District Licensed Victuallers Association passing a resolution requesting Col. Doyle to extend the hours in the Division from 9 to 10 p.m. It was pointed out there were no troops or munition works in the Division.

The Licensing Act of 1921 regularized this situation by defining 'permitted hours' as being eight hours between 11 a.m. and 10 p.m. except for Sunday, which was limited to five hours. In 1934, there was a slight improvement—an extension could be granted to 10.30 p.m. during the summer months, especially in rural areas where evening work was necessary.

After the Second World War there were several minor Acts, culminating in the 1961 Licensing Act which encouraged the proliferation of off-licences and provided for 'restaurant' licences. It also gave the customers' grace—the ten minutes of 'drinking-up time'. A late 20th-century Act restored the situation to more or less what it was at the beginning of the century, by allowing inns to stay open throughout most of the day if they so wish, most commonly any times between 11 a.m. and 11 p.m., with a somewhat shorter 'window of opportunity' on Sundays. A new millennium has brought new thought and it is most probable that restrictions upon public houses will be further reduced leading to the possibility of 24-hour opening once again.

Ludlow, which is crammed with 469 listed buildings, is reckoned to be one of the best preserved medieval plantation towns in Europe. According to J.B. Priestley in his *English Journey* of 1933, the town evokes the Old England of churches, manor houses, inns and teashops. So may it long remain or, in the words of A.E. Housman, whose ashes are buried in Ludlow churchyard, 'Till Ludlow tower is down'.

> Say, for what were hop-yards meant,
> Or why was Burton built on Trent?
> Oh many a peer of England brews
> Livelier liquor than the Muse,
> and malt does more than Milton can
> To justify God's ways to man.
> Ale, man, ale's the stuff to drink
> For fellows whom it hurts to think:
> Look into the pewter pot
> To see the world as the world's not.
> And faith, 'tis pleasant till 'tis past:
> The mischief is that 'twill not last.
>
> (*A Shropshire Lad*, A.E. Housman)

CHAPTER TWO

Brewing and Breweries

In George Farquhar's play *The Beaux' Stratagem* of 1707 Boniface, the landlord of an inn at Lichfield, tells a guest he has hardly ever eaten meat. 'I have fed purely upon ale, I have ate my ale, drank my ale, and I always sleep upon my ale'.

Ale, or beer, has been the staple drink in Britain since the introduction of grain. It was central to life, on an equal footing to bread, if not higher. The Romans found the Britons drinking fermented liquor made from barley and wheat. The Saxons and Danes, who followed, were great beer drinkers and brought more sophistication to the art of brewing. The Normans built castles and abbeys all over the country and every monastery had a brewery for the refreshment of monk and traveller. Brewing, like baking, was an essential part of housekeeping and ale was brewed in farmhouse, inn, and tavern.

Those engaged in brewing then were female, and ale-wives or brewsters, as they were known, were not held in very high esteeem. And God help the brewster who brewed bad ale or adulterated it. This heinous crime was punished by the ducking stool or even worse, as a misericord of the dishonest ale-wife in Ludlow's parish church illustrates. Carved on one of the stall seats in the choir is a rather chilling scene of demons and a terrified ale-wife, who has given short measure. Still clutching her deficient jug, she is

The 'dishonest ale-wife' misericord.

thrown over the shoulder of a demon while the Devil reads out her misdeeds from a long scroll. Another demon plays a bagpipe to serenade her journey to eternal damnation. Apparently the Ludlow ale-wife had been found guilty of lining her pots with pitch to give short measure. This is one of 28 misericords in the church all depicting medieval scenes, with the earliest carved in the late 14th century but most dating from 1447.

Punishment by ducking stool continued well into the 18th century with an ale-wife from Kingston ducked in 1745 and another from Chelmsford as late as 1801. Successive monarchs kept a keen eye on the price and a guaranteed supply of ale, which had become a necessity. Brewsters, therefore, could be punished for brewing less than they used to or for increasing their prices. The most famous ale-wife of England, however, was Elinour Rummin, of the Running Horse in Leatherhead, Surrey, who was immortalised in a ballad by John Skelton, poet laureate to Henry VIII. She is always depicted with two cups in her hands, the symbol of her trade. Later, when the profits to be made from brewing began to increase, men took over the role.

The biggest change in brewing came with the reintroduction of hops. The hop, *Humulus lupulus,* belongs to the *Cannabinacene* family of plants and was used by the Romans and throughout the medieval period as a delicacy (young hop shoots being prepared like asparagus) or for their medicinal purposes. Its value for preserving and flavouring beverages was known by the 12th century; their use in beer is probably of German origin. An anonymous rhyme dated 1520 observes 'Hops and turkeys, carp and beer, Came into England all in one year'. However, most authorities favour the year 1400 in a consignment from Holland. There were many people who objected, with a variety of reasons. Coming from the Low Countries it was considered by many to be a Protestant plant. Thus Andrew Boords, a physician, in his *Dyetary* of 1542 wrote: 'Beer is the natural drink for the Dutchman and recently it is much used in England to the detriment of the Englishman ... it killeth those who are troubled with collic and the stone ... it makes a man fat as shown by the Dutchman's faces and bellies'. The novelist Ford Madox Ford (1873-1939), put the following words in the mouth of a Kentish squire of Tudor times: 'The Almains call the plant "hopfen", but "hop" is a good enough word for me. From Bohemia come this goodly vine

The brewer, from a 16th-century woodcut.

that I am minded to plant in the county of Kent. With its aid is made that good drink that we call Brunswick Mum. But the Almains call it "bier", for it is made from the bere or barley plant. It is like our ale, but not so sweet'.

Henry VI is said to have prohibited brewers from using hops and many towns in England tried to prevent the brewing of beer by forbidding the use of hops— including Shrewsbury, where the use of the 'wicked weed' was banned in 1519. Hops, it was said, not only spoilt the taste of the drink, but endangered the lives of the people. However, the improvement made in the liquor by the new constituent came at last to be generally recognised and several hop gardens had been set up in Kent by the mid-16th century. Old prejudices survived and in 1630 Henry VIII instructed his brewer not to use hops or brimstone in his ale.

In *Drinke and Welcome*, John Taylor (1580-1653) had this to say:

Ale is rightly called Nappy for it will set a nap upon a mans threedbare eyes when he is sleepy. It is called Merry-goe-downe for it slides down merrily; It is fragrant to the sent; It is most pleasing to the taste; The flowring and mantling of it (like Chequer worke) with the Verdant smiling of it, is delightful to the sight, it is Touching or Feeling to the Braine and Heart; and (to please the senses all) it provokes men to singing and mirth, which is contenting to the Hearing.

And in Conclusion, it is such a nourisher of Mankinde, that if my mouth were as bigge as Bishopsgate, my Pen as long as a Maypole, and my Inke a flowring spring, or a standing fishpond, yet I could not with Mouth, Pen, or Inke, speak or write the true worth and worthinesse of Ale.

Burton upon Trent, Staffordshire, was home to some of the country's finest brewers including Ind Coope and Allsop which owned

An early 18th-century brewhouse.

some of the public houses in Ludlow. Burton's brewing tradition, aided by the calcium sulphate content of the local water, dated back to brewing by the Benedictine monks of Burton Abbey, founded in 1002. The Burton breweries were producing prime quality beers which were lighter and more bitter and began eroding the popularity of the London porter beers.

One of the basic ingredients of beer, both pale ale and stouts, is barley grains which have passed through the malting process to become maltose sugars. Malting as a trade became of growing importance in Ludlow with the number of malting businesses increasing from 18 in 1770 to 30 in 1828. There were many malthouses, especially in Corve Street, using barley which was grown in Shropshire. Hops were another ingredient readily available, there being a hop market in Mill Street selling locally-grown and Worcester varieties.

Until the middle of the 19th century most landlords made their own ale and beer in small brewhouses behind their inns. However, many of the smaller inns and beer-houses that opened during the first half of the 19th century had no brewing facilities and were dependent on other inns or on the growing number of breweries for their supply. The main brewery in Ludlow was the **Ludlow and Craven Arms Brewery** Co Ltd, situated in Corve Street, which produced many a well crafted beer. An advert of 1844 proclaimed:

> The reason the Ales produced at this brewery are of such a thorough Home Brewed Character is because they are Brewed from the finest Shropshire barley and Worcester hops, only, and guaranteed free from any adulteration.
>
> The Amber Bitter Ale is a speciality of this Brewery, it is a fine light bitter ale, with a thoroughly Home Brewed flavour. To be had in casks 9, 18, 36 and 54 gallons.

This advert was nothing to the one which appeared in the *Ludlow Advertiser* of 26 January 1901. Headed 'Ludlow and Craven Arms Brewery Analysis of Beers and Stout' it reproduced a copy of a letter from The Laboratory, Bath Row, Birmingham:

Dear Sirs,
We duly received your samples carrying prefix marks as follows: No 8 AK Light Dinner Ale, No 14 Amber Bitter Ale, No 15 XX Ale, No 16 AK Ale, No 18 XX Ale, Single Stout.

The beers had evidently been produced from Malt and Hops and passed careful and exhaustive examination as PURE, NUTRITIVE and entirely free from any deleterious matter. Remaining for some little time at Laboratory Temperature the beers became quite brilliant and sparkling, so should prove wholesome beverages when distributed in the trade.

Believe me,
    yours faithfully
        Frank Faulkner,
        Consulting Brewer; assisted by William Duncan FIC, FCS

Two years later another advertisement, this time for Special Harvest Beer at 6d. per gallon, contained an extract from a Report of the Public Analyst for Shropshire: 'The water is of exceptional purity as regards organic matter, and well fitted for brewing'.

The front pages of the *Ludlow Advertiser* for the first five months of 1911 contained more Ludlow and Craven Arms Brewery adverts such as 'Home Brewed Ales from 8d. to 1s. 4d. per gallon—Extra Oatmeal Stout 1s. 2d. per gallon—Bottles Department—Ludlow Golden Ale—Oatmeal Stout'. In June that year there was a change in the advertising to commemorate the accession of George V, the second son of Edward VII, to the throne with 'The Coronation Ale—A magnificent brew'. This attempt at special ales must have been successful for December saw a change to 'The Christmas Ale—A special Brew'.

The brewery owned four public houses: the **Trotting Horse** in Corve Street, the **Blue Boar** and **Hop Pole** in Mill Street and the **Star**. When the **Hop Pole** ceased trading as a pub the premises were used as the brewery's wine and spirit department. In the early 1930s the site of

A late 19th century advertisement for the Ludlow Brewery.

the Brewery in Corve Street was acquired for the construction of the New Bromfield Road (renamed Coronation Avenue). Its houses were taken over by the Shrewsbury brewers, Trouncers, who in turn were taken over by Ind Coope in 1964.

Breweries throughout the country were closing at an alarming rate. In 1900 there were some 6,390, a number which steadily fell until 70 years later there were fewer than 200 in the country. Pasteurised sterile beer, known as keg, and lager were taking over, which together soon accounted for the majority of beer sales. Beer brewed at individual inns almost ceased with only a handful of examples surviving such as the Three Tuns in Bishop's Castle, which has been brewing since 1642, and the All Nations in Madeley. Both breweries have since closed, but in recent years nine independent breweries have begun operations in Shropshire making this a county rich in beers of the home brewed kind, such as Shropshire Lad, Big Nev's, and XXX Bitter. The new breweries are the Salopian and Dolphin, Shrewsbury; Hanby, Wem; Six Bells, Bishop's Castle; Hobsons, Cleobury Mortimer; Wood, Wistanstow; Corvedale, Corfton; the Munslow, Munslow; and Worfield, Bridgnorth. All these will benefit from the reduction in duty on the products of small breweries announced by the Chancellor in his budget of April 2002.

With the increase of locally produced beer, however, has come the virtual demise of the national brewing industry as far as real ale is concerned following a series of mergers and takeovers. Now the industry is concentrated in the hands of a few global giants while pub groups are owned by German and Japanese banks.

18

CHAPTER THREE

The Castle, Dinham & Mill Street

The history of Ludlow really began to develop with the building of the castle by Roger de Lacy 20 years after the Norman Conquest. A town was then laid out in a rectilinear grid outside the castle gates in an angled bend of the River Teme. Later, stone walls including nine gateways were built to surround the town. Trading in wool and cloth, Ludlow became prosperous in the Middle Ages.

Over the years Ludlow Castle has been associated with many royal personages, but all were ill-fated. After having Edward II murdered in Berkeley Castle, Roger (IV) Mortimer entertained Queen Isabella and the infant Edward III at Ludlow Castle in 1328. For two years Mortimer ruled England in the name of Edward's son until the latter in due course had him beheaded. The son of the last Mortimer was Richard, duke of York, the leader of the Yorkist faction in the Wars of the Roses. Ludlow was thus involved in the Wars, and was sacked by the Lancastrians in 1459, when looting soldiers went 'footshode in wine'. After the 'battle' of Ludford Bridge, when the duke of York deserted his forces overnight, Ludlow was given over to pillaging by the royal forces, as was the Carmelite Friary, but there seems to have been little structural damage to buildings. According to one contemporary, the king's men, 'when they hadde drokyn i-nowe of wyne that was in tavernys and in othyr placys they tulle ungoodely smote owte the heddys of the pypys and hoggys hedys of wyne, that men wente wete-schede in wyne, and thenn they robbyd the towne, and bare a-awaye beddynge and clothe and othyr stuffe and defoulyd many wymmen'.

Fortunes were reversed when Richard's son became king as Edward IV, for he rewarded loyal Ludlow with its charter of incorporation as a borough, confirming many ancient privileges.

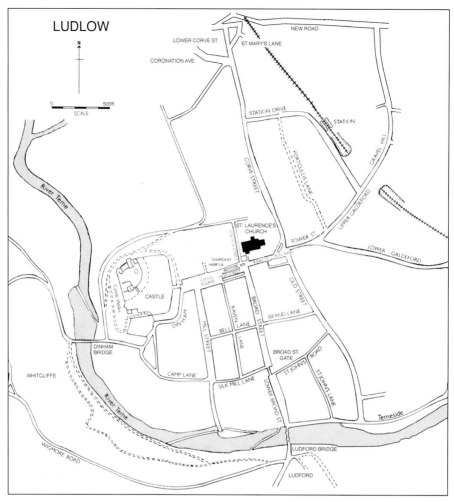

LUDLOW

N

0   500ft.
SCALE

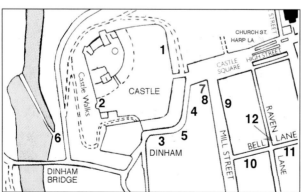

The Castle, Dinham and Mill Street.

1—Ludlow Castle
2—Mortimer's Tower
3—Welsh Harp
4—Harp
5—Dinham Hall *
6—Mr. Underhill's *
7—Hop Pole
8—Blue Boar *
9—Three Tuns
10—Coach & Horses
11—Swan
12—Bell
*—Open in 2002

Edward V (1470-83) and his younger brother, Richard—the little princes later murdered in the Tower of London—spent most of their boyhood at Ludlow. Then Prince Arthur (1486-1502), elder son of Henry VII, came to Ludlow with his bride, Catherine of Aragon. They spent six months at the castle before Arthur died of 'sweating sickness', his heart (some say his bowels) being buried in Ludlow parish church, and the remainder of his body in Worcester Cathedral.

Mary Tudor (1515-58), who became queen in 1553, as a young girl spent the winters of 1525/6 and 1526/7 at Ludlow. She was known as 'Bloody Mary' after re-introducing the heresy laws in her attempt to restore Roman Catholicism in England.

Crown ownership and geographical position made the castle an ideal headquarters for the Council in the Marches of Wales, which was established in 1475 and administered Wales and the border counties until 1689, except for periods in the Civil War and Commonwealth. For the whole of that period Ludlow was virtually the capital of Wales and the border counties.

Not surprisingly Ludlow was then a bustling place, which appeared to have been notorious for both the number of its inns and the number of lawyers in the early 17th century. A certain Richard Baxter, when a youth, lived as a pupil with the chaplain of the Council in Ludlow Castle, and in his memoirs, *Reliquiae Baxterianae,* he alluded to the licentiousness of the place: 'About 17 years of age, being at Ludlow castle, where many idle gentlemen had little else to do, I had a mind to learn to play at tables; and the best gamester in the house undertook to teach me'. Baxter went on: 'The house was great (there being four judges, the king's attorney, the secretary, the clerk of the fines, with all their servants, and all the lord president's servants, and many more) and the town was full of temptations, through the multitude of persons (councillors, attorneys, officers and clerks) and much given to tippling and excess'.

At an early date there was a brewhouse in the castle's inner bailey. In the Great Tower court, a service area, there was a brewhouse set against the curtain wall protecting the inner bailey, built between 1086 and 1094. A well and the remains of a drying kiln are still visible.

There was also an inn called the **Castle** near the outer bailey, which existed in the 18th and early 19th centuries, and as the **Ludlow**

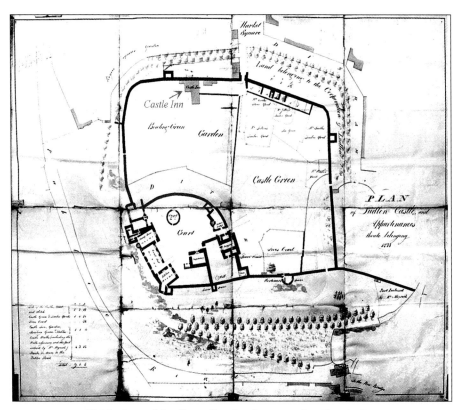

*1811 plan of Ludlow Castle showing the **Castle Inn**
and the Bowling Green.*

Castle it was first recorded in 1744. The inn, which was part of a house that occupied the site of a 'fayre tennys corte' built in 1658, had a bowling green and gardens extending from near the existing gatehouse to the inner bailey curtain wall, just to the east of the Judges' Lodgings. Much of the present outer bailey was then used as timber yards. The inn was eventually closed and became part of a gentleman's residence which was extended several times. In the 1950s the building was converted into flats, but it is hoped that it will soon be used as part of the amenities of the castle.

Then there was **Mortimer's Castle**, a mug-house on the outer wall. A mug-house was an 18th-century ale-house, so called because it was where many people gathered in a large tap-room to drink, sing and spout. Ale was served to the company in their own mugs, and the place where the mug was to stand was chalked on the table. The 'house' was included in a list of inns for the Castle Street ward of

22

*The right-hand section was probably part of the **Castle Inn**.
Taken from the garden in 2002.*

1792 and was described by George Nicholson in his *Cambrian Traveller's Guide* of 1813:

> This tower (Mortimer's) is ignominiously occupied as a mug-house, the ancient windows of which have been supplied with modern enlarged square ones, stuck in without order, obtruding on every beholder a glaring effigy of depraved taste. If the proprietor would allow it, a small subscription of the inhabitants might speedily rescue this venerable tower from the gross barbarism of reform, by substituting windows adapted to the prevailing architecture of the building. The side of this tower facing the town exhibits no windows but has been adapted to a Fives'-court.

It would appear then that rather than providing just refreshment for the Fives' players, it served drinks to people promenading outside the castle along the public walk which the Countess of Powis commissioned in 1772. Fives was apparently a popular sport, and in 1788 there was a notice: 'A Match at Fives to be played at the Fives Court in Ludlow, on the 28th day of August, being the second Race Day, in the Morning for Twenty Guineas, Shropshire against Breconshire'.

Late night revellers may well have caught a glimpse of one of the castle's several ghosts including the sad 12th-century figure of Marion

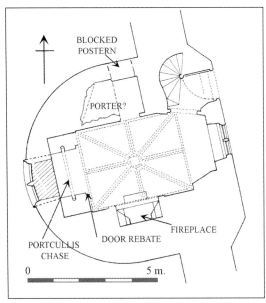

*Mortimer's Tower — **The Mug House**.*
Upper : Ground floor plan.
Lower : From the public walk.

de la Bruyère who, after inadvertently betraying the castle and then slaying her treacherous lover, leapt to her death from the Pendover Tower.

Another intriguing spectacle would have been witnessed on 3 September, 1828 when a Mr. Greening ascended in a hot air balloon from the Castle Green. He apparently descended at Congleton in Cheshire 75 miles away.

To the south of the castle lies Dinham, an area leading down towards the river, where Ludlow's first dwellings were probably built. Over the years there have been at least four inns by the name of **Harp** and two of them were in Dinham. Records first mention a Dinham **Harp** in 1615 and then again in 1742. Records also show that a messuage called the **Welsh Harp** was in possession of the Collier family from 1702 till 1813. James Collier converted it into two houses about 1744, one of which retained the Welsh Harp name. A third house was added at the western end. Between 1808 and 1810 the houses were altered and repaired and later sold to John Jones and Robert Smallman, who purchased No. 14. Apart from alterations to the windows, this fine 17th-century timber-framed house, decorated with diagonals and star

24

panels, survives to this day and is still called the Welsh Harp, a sign of which it proudly displays.

*The **Welsh Harp** in 2001.*

There was another **Harp** at the residential property of No. 7 Dinham of which the oldest part dates back to the 15th century. It is not known how long the building served as the **Harp** in the 15th and 16th centuries, but it probably consisted simply of a front parlour selling beer. There used to be a front door behind the street wall where there is now a verandah, and along that side of the house was a first-floor jetty. However, during Victorian/Regency times the area underneath the jetty was infilled to enlarge the living room area, although there is still a jetty on the other side of the house. The front door now goes through what used to be the front room or the bar area, leaving a rather grand fireplace in what is now the

*No. 7 Dinham; once the **Harp**.*

hall. Timberwork has been stuccoed, a brick façade constructed at the end of the 18th century, and French and sash windows installed. The stable block and pigeon loft at the rear are probably still the original. In one of the bedrooms there is a beam which has writing in Welsh.

In between the two **Harps** stands the impressive looking **Dinham Hall**, on the site of which used to be an 18th-century inn called the **Hole in the Wall**. The name was perhaps an allusion to a prison's hole

Dinham Hall in 2002.

in the wall through which the inmates received donations, or, as is more likely in this case, a reference to the narrow alley by which the tavern was approached. Yet another alternative derivation may be because the newly laid-out castle walks, blocked by the grounds of Dinham House, were re-routed through two openings cut through the castle's curtain wall.

It was a private house, lying between two gardens in Dinham (East), when a Ludlow widow, Jane Morgan, and her son, William Morgan, a glover from Leominster, were granted a lease for the property in 1726 from Ludlow Corporation. The name **Hole in the Wall** is given for the first time in 1755, but apparently the house had been an inn for some time. The Corporation leased it up until 1789. The northern boundary of the **Hole in the Wall** included a passage that led from Dinham into the yard of the **Blue Boar Inn** in Mill Street.

Re-built in 1792 by Samuel Nash as a spacious town house faced with stone, **Dinham Hall** was a private residence for many years. Then in 1894 it was rented out at £40 a year to house the headmaster of Ludlow Grammar School and his 26 boarders. It was bought in 1961 and in 1977 became Hall of Residence for Ludlow College. Some time later it became a hotel in the country house style with a well regarded restaurant.

Close to the banks of the river Teme is **Mr. Underhill's at Dinham Weir**, which was converted from the premises of one of the castle mills where corn was ground in the Middle Ages. At the beginning of the 21st century it is described as 'a restaurant with rooms' and holds the English Tourism Council silver award, but in 1992 it was described merely as a hotel and restaurant.

On the east side of Dinham, leading from Castle Square south to the Teme, is Mill Street. By the 16th century the top end of the street was known as the Shambles—used not for slaughtering, but for butchers' shops, six of them in two rows with lofts above. There had been an earlier Shambles in the High Street where animals were slaughtered with meat vendors using tables called shambles. The Mill Street Shambles were finally cleared in 1739. Within a few years a hop market had been opened further down the street, which became one of the main centres for the sale of locally-grown hops, providing this necessary ingredient to the brewers who served the 50 pubs in Ludlow at the beginning of the 20th century.

On the west side of Mill Street going south were two inns side by side, of which only one still exists. The first one, at No. 53, now housing a firm of chartered accountants, was called the **Hop Pole** (the hop vines were then trained up hop poles rather than as today onto wires). It was originally called the **Swan**, first mentioned in records of 1541, though its next mention is in 1749 in connection with neighbouring No. 54. Part of the property, which was settled on the marriage of Henry Karver, an attorney, and Theophila Edmunds comprised:

a.   The **Swan**, in Mill Street near the Shambles, as let by Simon Vaughan to Roger Jones in 1647;

b,   A messuage, garden, brewhouse, shop and stables, formerly messuages. This property extended from another messuage along Mill Street and Castle Street into Dinham to a messuage late of Edward Wood, gentleman; and had been let by the Corporation to Benjamin Karver in 1736.

c.   A messuage in the Shambles with slaughterhouses and yard, with Karver's messuage.

By 1776 the top house was occupied by Ann Syer, widow, an under-tenant to Theophila Karver, whose husband had died. The Shambles had gone and in their place were three houses erected by Karver between the top house and the **Swan**. In 1790 John Glaze was the innkeeper and in 1792 it was mentioned in a list of inns. But by 1800 it was called the **Hop Pole**, being described at that time as being a timber-framed building with jetty and twin dormers.

In 1826 George Anderson, a Ludlow gentleman and tenant of one of the three new houses, persuaded Mary McGhie, tenant of the top house, to sell him part of her stable yard and brewhouse. He agreed to build a dividing wall across the yard and to erect a new brewhouse and privy on her side. Ale purchased from the inn on 9 March 1827 was described as 'good, bad and indifferent'. In 1838 the Corporation granted Anderson two leases—the first of a house in Mill Street between a house of Henry Ruddall, occupied by Miss Waring, and the **Hop Pole Inn**, and the second of a stable, brewhouse and yard in Dinham. Under his will Anderson's trustees sold No. 54 in 1867.

John Weames was landlord in 1859 and Jane Ingram in 1888. In 1901 a valuation was made of 'the blinds, shed and licences', by

George Hagan to the Ludlow and Craven Arms Brewery Co., and in a return of licensed houses of the same year, the **Hop Pole** was shown as being owned by the brewery with John Smith Leake as occupier. It consisted of a bar, kitchen and four bedrooms. There was no stabling. By this time it had ceased trading as an inn and was now the brewery's main wholesale and retail outlet for wines and spirits with the premises used as stores and offices. In 1915 it was called **Ye Olde Hop Pole**.

In the 1920s it was sold and transformed into one of the first garages in Ludlow. Around this time a functions room was built between the garage and the **Blue Boar** and was used

*The **Hop Pole** is occupied by a firm of accountants in 2001.*

regularly by the Ludlow Town Band up until the mid-1990s. The **Hop Pole** has since had a face lift and is occupied by a firm of accountants.

Next door at No. 52 is the **Blue Boar**, a commodious inn that was built in the 17th century as a large house with imposing brick chimneys. Later it became an inn called the **Portcullis**—a name apparently derived from its proximity to the gatehouse of the Guildhall enclosure just further down the road. Heraldically it referred to Henry VII and Henry VIII.

Since 1739 the inn has been called the **Blue Boar**, although there was a **Boare** listed in 1633. The name usually refers to Richard III who was known as the Boar, a nickname derived from his heraldic white boar. He was just seven when taken prisoner with his mother by the Lancastrians when they captured Ludlow Castle in 1459. Many inns known as the White Boar were quickly changed to Blue Boar after the

defeat of Richard and the Yorkists at the Battle of Bosworth, for the blue boar was a heraldic emblem of the Earl of Oxford, a leading supporter of the Lancastrian cause.

Richard Wigley was the innkeeper in 1790. The **Blue Boar** is mentioned in a book called *The History of Susan Gray*, written in 1802 by Mrs. Mary Sherwood. Intended for the 'benefit of young women when going to service', it claimed to be the first book especially written to inculcate religious principles in the poor. Susan was maid to an elderly woman living near Ludlow. An acquaintance tells her: 'The soldiers are in town, I suppose you know that. You may hear the drums and fifes down here very plain; and we had a dance yesterday at the **Blue-Boar**. My mother and I were both there; and the long room was so full, that you could hardly squeeze in; and the women were all so smart'! In 1837 the **Blue Boar** was described as including the **Hop Pole** inn, two adjoining Corporation messuages and the Guildhall, together with a garden and a street leading into Dinham with another Corporation messuage.

*The **Blue Boar** about 1900.*

*The **Blue Boar** (central) and the **Hop Pol**e (right) in 1960.*

In 1844 the proprietor was in an ill state of health which obliged him to retire. Ten years later the new innkeeper was William Pea, who was taking a man to court. The *Ludlow Advertiser* of 15 March 1856 reported: 'Pea v Cox—claim £1 2s. The plaintiff was landlord of the **Blue Boar** and the defendant a sub-bailiff of the county court at the time the debt was contracted. Ordered to pay 4s. a month. County Court, March 13'.

Thirty years later the **Blue Boar** was in the news again with the *Ludlow Advertiser* of 15 August, 1885 reporting a 'Brutal assault'. The report went on:

> Samuel Bridges was charged on a warrant with committing a violent assault on Valentine Cox, at the **Blue Boar Inn**. The complainant said in company of Bridges and two other men I went to the **Plough Inn** and had a quart of beer. Bridges and witness went to the **Blue Boar Inn**, where Bridges insisted upon having a pipe belonging to witness to smoke with, and while Bridges was smoking witness knocked the pipe with his stick, upon which Bridges knocked Cox down, and severely kicked him in the ribs when on the floor. Two servants at the **Blue Boar** corroborated witness's statement. Several previous convictions were put in against the prisoner, who was sentenced to 28 days imprisonment with hard labour.

By 1888 Mary Davies was described as a licensed victualler and brewer. A year later the **Blue Boar** was in danger of being closed down. The Borough Magistrates objected to the renewal of its licence on the grounds that the licensee did not live on the premises and that the inn was not required for the wants of the neighbourhood. 'After a long hearing, with complex comparisons between the stabling facilities of the **Blue Boar** and the **George**, and much evidence on the importance of the **Blue Boar** to the farming community, the magistrates withdrew their objection'. In 1894 a case was brought for selling ale and whisky without a license, but it was dismissed on payment of costs. The return of licensed houses for 1901 showed that it was tied to the Brewery with George Hogan as the occupier. It consisted of a bar, parlour, smokeroom, two kitchens and six bedrooms. Hogan had been there since at least 1894. There was stabling for nine horses.

*The **Blue Boar** in 2002.*

Trade was described as 'agricultural and in town'.

It was during that year that the inn was sold to the Ludlow and Craven Arms Brewery Company, when a schedule of the landlord's fixtures made for the brewery included 'a five pull beer engine and pipes to cellars and taps complete'.

The present building is one of the first in Ludlow to be built of brick, locally made, as indicated by the chimney stacks. In the mid-1950s the inn was renowned for its beer-drinking jackdaw—Jack. He was the pet of

Mrs. Bert Hope, the licensee's wife, and lived in a cage in the stone-flagged inn yard. According to the *Ludlow Advertiser* of 9 December, 1954: 'On slack nights he is allowed into the bar and gurgles back ale from pint glasses'. Today the inn is owned by Pubmaster and continues its long connection with the Ludlow Festival. It still has its impressive chimneys and an alley leading through to Dinham. According to the present landlord, Mr. Phil Unwin, the **Blue Boar** is host to three ghosts: an old man who smokes a clay pipe, a woman associated with a local school, and a cavalier who is said to inhabit the whole street. Ghostly happenings he has experienced include beer taps inexplicably turning on and off and a 19 gallon beer barrel moving from one side of the cellar to the other.

On the other side of the road, opposite the Guildhall, was an inn called the **Three Tuns**, probably at No. 4 and 4a. This is now a large, three-storey private house with the remnants of a beer cellar at the front and a gateway leading to rear garages which were originally stables. The inn is mentioned in lists for 1775 and 1792 and in 1790 the inn-keeper was named as Mrs. Rollins. Robert Jones was the landlord in 1859. It would seem that the inn then changed its name to the **White Horse** (one is mentioned in a directory of 1863) taking the name of the original **White Horse** a few doors away on the corner with Castle Street, which was demolished in 1840. But this too had gone by the 1870s. Until the 1980s it was a private hotel.

As in other parts of Ludlow, Mill Street was the home of malthouses as well as inns. Thus an auction in 1821 comprised 'a large and handsome dwelling in Mill Street fit for the reception of a genteel family with a large building adjoining, lately used as a Malthouse'.

Half way down Mill Lane on the east side is Bell

*The **Three Tuns** in 2002.*

33

Coach and Horses in 2001.

Lane which leads through to Broad Street. At No. 4 there used to be an inn called the **Coach & Horses**, which is shown on a map of Ludlow dated 1835. The licensee is given as Hugh Greenhouse in a directory of 1859, but by 1885 he is described simply as a carpenter at the same address.

Further along, at No. 10, was the **Swan**, flying again after the name had been lost in 1800 to the **Hop Pole** in Mill Street. In a directory of 1859 the licensee is named as William Davis. But the **Swan** did not trade for very long and closed in the early 1880s. The three-storey property still retains a cellar, while the bar area has been converted into a sitting room and dining room. The name, perpetuated in 'Swan House', probably came from the badge of Henry IV after marrying Mary de Bohun, and later from that of Henry VI. It is also said to have been favoured by Edward III and Henry VIII. A swan is featured in one of the misericords in St. Laurence's church.

*The **Swan** in Bell Lane in 2001.*

Another inn called the **Bell** (of which it has been said 'it speaks all languages') was thriving in the 17th century at No. 21 Bell Lane. In 1626 it was recorded in the list of 16 inns which showed an inn sign and was therefore one of the leading hostelries in Ludlow. Situated opposite Swan House, the **Bell** no longer exists. In its place stands an imposing three-storey house with an integral garage.

CHAPTER FOUR

Castle Square & Church Street

'At Ludlow', a writer noted in 1828, 'the beauties of Herefordshire and Shropshire meet together in hilarity and display their rival beauties to the admiring swains; the land of cider and the land of beef send their sons hither'.

These beauties and swains probably congregated in Castle Square, then, as now, the town's focal point. The square was then dominated by the Market Hall, built in 1702 and serving as a corn market with commodious assembly rooms over it for Corporation meetings and balls.

The square was usually a hive of activity, even more so on special days of the year such as Shrove Tuesday when one of the most remarkable of Ludlow's many traditional customs was held—the grand 'tug-of-war' between the inhabitants of Castle and Broad Street wards and Corve and Old Street wards. Described as 'an uncouth practice', this rope-pulling attracted boisterous crowds and usually ended in drunkenness and disorder. Shops were shut at 4 o'clock when a rope 3 inches thick and 36 yards long, with a knob at each end, one blue the other red, was given out by the mayor from one of the Market Hall's upper floor windows. Waiting for the rope were two old ladies, sitting on the shoulders of two men, representing the two teams. Dangling the rope out of the window, the mayor would by custom suddenly retrieve it, often causing one or both of the women to topple to the ground, much to the amusement of the crowd.

When the rope had been finally secured by one of the contestants, the pulling began with the teams often being lost among the mob of sightseers who included 'lawyers and their clerks, tradesmen, gentlemen and even parsons, all prepared to give a push

35

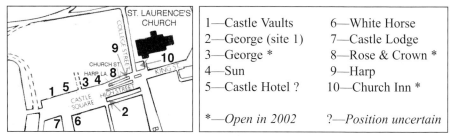

1—Castle Vaults	6—White Horse
2—George (site 1)	7—Castle Lodge
3—George *	8—Rose & Crown *
4—Sun	9—Harp
5—Castle Hotel ?	10—Church Inn *
*—Open in 2002	?—Position uncertain

Castle Square & Church Street.

if not a pull, and a queer looking set they were when it was all over —all rags and tatters'.

An arduous struggle ensued. If the contest was carried down Mill Street, the Red Knob party had won and they dipped the knobs in the river Teme in token of victory. If it was carried into the Bull Ring, the Blue Knob team was victorious. The rope was then taken back to the Market Hall and given out again. If the same team won again, the contest was over, but if the opposite side won, a third and final pull would decide the winners. 'Then the rope was sold, the money got for it spent in beer, and fighting and quarrelling commenced'.

These disorderly scenes and the dangerous accidents which often happened during the tug-of-war, caused it to be discontinued in 1851. Although regarded as a carnival game, this singular custom may have commemorated the battle of Ludford Bridge, when the townspeople were divided into White and Red Rose parties and much bloodshed took place in the town. One of the town bailiffs headed the Red Rose party and lost his life in attempting to open Dinham Gate to King Henry VI.

The Market Hall, which had apparently reached the end of its useful life, was replaced by the Town Hall, built in the 1880s to a design by Henry Cheers of Twickenham at a cost of about £6,000. Later this building was described by Nikolaus Pevsner as 'Ludlow's bad luck', adding 'There is nothing that could be said in favour of its fiery brick or useless Elizabethan detail'. The Town Hall lasted a hundred years before, in 1986, it too was demolished. Different sentiments were accorded by local historian David Lloyd who described its demise as 'arguably the saddest Ludlow event of the century'. Nothing has replaced the building.

There were, of course, numerous inns and taverns in which the revellers could slake their thirst, including several in the Square itself.

Castle Square shortly before the Market Hall was demolished in 1887.
*The **George Inn** is evident on the left with E. Butcher as licensee.*

On the north side, situated four doors on the castle side of the present **George** and close to Ludlow College, was the 19th-century **Castle Vaults**. It lived up to its name (premises where wines and other liquors were stored) by selling wines and spirits in addition to ales and porter.

Castle Square about 1900, with the Town Hall just left of centre.
*The **George** is again on the left.*

One licensee, Edward Powell, also advertised himself as 'plumber, painter and glazier'. **Castle Vaults** is marked on an Ordnance Survey map of 1884. Towards the end of the 20th century the building suffered from serious structural problems and eventually had to be demolished.

Further down, on the corner of the road that now leads to the car park, is the **George**, an inn that was originally on the other side of the Square, at 8 High Street, on the corner where it joins Market Street. When restorations were made there in 1979 substantial remains of a 16th–century building with a half-timbered exterior were found. This **George**, probably named after St. George, the patron saint of England, was among the first half dozen inns recorded in Ludlow. It is first mentioned in a list of inns of 1559 and in 1626 it is listed as among the 16 inns known by their signs. It was some time early in the 18th century that it moved to its present site. In the 19th century the High Street premises were owned by James and Edward Harding and more recently as a store run by Foster Brothers, then YP. It is now a country clothing shop with two floors of offices above.

*The **Castle Vaults** (No. 18) in 1990.*

*The **George** was originally across the Square at 8 High Street.*

One of the first innkeepers listed at the new **George Inn** was John Jay in 1790. At the beginning of the next century the **George** was one of Ludlow's principal inns and also a depot for the carriers' trade. Country people used to walk or ride into market, many of them by the carriers' carts which serviced neighbouring villages, and terminated at pubs such as the **George**. There were then some 13 departures a week from the inn going to such places as Adforton,

A peaceful 1960s scene in Ludlow, with the ***George Hotel*** *on the right and part of the Town Hall on the left.*

Bush Mill, Bridgnorth, Munslow, Brimfield, Culmington, Munslow Aston and Orlton's Common. The inn was also a favourite meeting place for farmers and lads, particularly on a market or auction Monday when the sheep and cattle from all around Ludlow were driven in for sale.

In 1859 the name of the inn was changed to the **George and Dragon** with James Bach as licensee (the name Dragon was obviously in vogue then as there were also two **Green Dragons**, one in Old Street and the other in Corve Street), then in 1868 the 'Dragon' was dropped and by 1876 the inn was run by William Butcher, licensee and brewer. He was apparently a keen angler, but in July of that year he caught more than he bargained for. He was fishing in the Teme at Burway when he found the body of a drowned young man. An inquest later established that the body was that of 28-year-old Grantley Lee Powell, who had been staying in Ludlow a few weeks and was suffering from epilepsy.

*The **George** in 2002.*

By 1888, the licensee and brewer was Elizabeth Butcher, presumably Butcher's widow, who supplied the supper at the first ball for the new Town Hall on 9 November 1889. According to the *Ludlow Advertiser:* 'a magnificent spread was put before the 250 guests' comprising: 'roast beef, braised beef, galantine of veal, hams and tongues, galantine of turkeys, roast turkeys, roast fowls, raised game pies, galantine of fowls, roast lamb, roast ducks, veal and ham pies, lobster salads, roast pheasants, roast partridges. Champagne and clarets were also served'.

Mrs. Butcher later blotted her copybook. On 21 January 1896, she was charged with selling adulterated whisky and ordered to pay costs of £1 10s. including an analyst's fee of 21s. However, the return of licensed houses in 1901 showed that she was still running the **George Hotel**. At that time it comprised a bar parlour, two kitchens, a sitting room, club room and eight bedrooms. There was stabling for 20 horses and it was described as a 'good market house'. The inn continued to boast of having the largest livery stables in Ludlow, with accommodation for up to 40 horses, until after the Second World War.

The 1926 *Kelly's Directory* listed Joseph Kind as landlord and the directory of 1941 showed that he was still there. As recently as 1958 the **George**, and elsewhere in Ludlow, still accepted brass tokens, valued at one-and-a-half pennies, in exchange for a half pint of beer. At the beginning of the 21st century the **George** is owned by Pubmaster.

Next to the **George**, at 10 Castle Street, was the **Sun** which had closed by the 1870s when it was at least a century old. Early inn signs for pubs of this name consisted of a simple circle with perhaps a few rays surrounding it and possibly a face painted in the circle. A **Sun** is mentioned in a list of pubs for 1742 and again in 1792. The innkeeper was given as Edward Grub in 1790, and at the beginning of the 19th century it was listed as one of Ludlow's principal inns. It might have been the inn called the **Woodbine** at one stage, for Thomas Rocke, its innkeeper, was described as landlord of the neighbouring inn to the

*The archway once led to the stables at the rear of the **Sun Inn**.*

George. Rocke moved to the **Feathers** in 1806, staying there until 1812. A **Woodbine** in Castle Street is also listed in 1840. The name has nothing to do with early cigarettes! It was originally used for several climbing plants and in early times was used for the convulvulus and ivy. It is now restricted to the common honeysuckle.

In 1817 the landlord of the **Sun** bought a slaughter-house, formerly a stable, and a small yard, once a pigsty, in Quality Square which adjoins Castle Street. In the same year two posters appeared, both of which may have related to the **Sun**. The first one simply stated: 'A Convenient Public House to be let, and entered upon at Lady Day, 1817. For particulars, apply to Mr. John Harper, Castle Street, Ludlow'. Another poster appeared in April, but unfortunately there is no indication of the inn's location. From the description, however, it could well have been the **Sun**. It read:

> Advantageous offer. To be let (with immediate possession) an old accustomed Public House, now in full business comprising — a lofty kitchen, 17 ft by 14, Parlour 24 ft by 12, Pantry and scullery, 4 good bed rooms, two of them large enough for 3 beds each, excellent arched cellar, capacious and convenient Brewhouse, with a 152 gallon copper furnace, and a small iron ditto. Two stables and hay-loft, large yard with driving way.
>
> N.B. The ale and beer which is of the first quality and successive age, to be taken at a fair valuation. Likewise the barrels, brewing utensils and part of the household furniture.

An auction of a freehold house was held at the **Sun Inn** in 1842. *Slater's Royal National and Commercial Directory for Shropshire* in 1859 listed the **Sun's** innkeeper as William Sheppard. But there is no mention of a **Sun** in the *Slater's Directory of Shropshire* for 1868.

CASTLE HOTEL, THE
SQUARE, LUDLOW.

H. CARTER,

COOK AND CONFECTIONER.

CATERER FOR DINNERS,
BALL SUPPERS,
COLD LUNCHEONS, AND
WEDDING BREAKFASTS.

Parties Supplied with all kinds of Refreshments.

PURE CALVES' FEET JELLY

For INVALIDS, packed either in Bottles or Moulds, and sent to any part to suit Customers.

VANILLA AND STRAWBERRY ICE CREAM.
PINE APPLE AND LEMON ICE WATER
of the first quality supplied on the Shortest Notice.

TERMS STRICTLY MODERATE.

AGENT FOR—

T. & W. T. SOUTHAM'S
CELEBRATED SHROPSHIRE ALES
AND
WATKINS' DUBLIN STOUT
FOR INVALIDS.

HALF BOTTLES, 2/- Per Dozen.

Advertisement of 1890.

The premises were used for a time after the First World War by the Comrades of the Great War, a local forerunner of the British Legion. It then became shops of various kinds— gunsmiths, butchers, ironmongers— and is now a Kwik Save supermarket. There is still an archway leading to the rear and the stables were at one time used as a fish and chip shop.

There also seems to have been a **Castle Hotel** in Castle Square. *Porter's Directory of Salop* for 1888 has an entry to this effect with a Henry Carter in charge. He was described as a licensed victualler, cook and confectioner. This is reinforced by an advertisement in the *Ludlow Advertiser* of 1 February 1890 about the Castle Hotel and H. Carter, cook & confectioner.

On the corner of Castle Street and Mill Street once stood the **White Horse**, an ancient hostelry occupying part of the Assembly Rooms, with a smithy near to it in Mill Street. It was a handsome timber-framed building featuring 11 chimney stacks (recorded in documents of 1668) and which once had a jetty subsequently underpinned with brick or stone walls. The earliest reference to the **White Horse** is in 1539, one of Ludlow's first inns to be recorded, and there are other mentions in 1743 and 1792. In 1790 the innkeepers were named as Ann and Edward Leake. The premises were apparently used as a private residence during the 17th century when it was occupied by a series of important tradesmen such as John Reynolds, a mercer who was twice town bailiff. On 16 December 1826, a meeting was held there to form an Association for the Prosecution of Felons.

The building was demolished in 1840 to make way for new Assembly Rooms, large enough to hold balls for up to 800 people, and including a Museum of Natural History, a subscribers Reading Room, and various offices. The following year a public ball was held there to celebrate the birth of Her Royal Highness, the Princess Royal. The Rooms later became the Starline Club, a cinema, and then a multi-purpose arts and cinema centre. It now also houses the Ludlow Museum and Tourist Information Centre.

CASTLE LODGE HOTEL
LUDLOW
Castle Square, Castle Lodge on right. Reproduction from an ancient etching

Castle Lodge on right, with the White Horse on left, from an old postcard.

Castle Lodge in 2001.

On the other side of Mill Street stands the impressive 15th-century **Castle Lodge**. It bulges with wooden panelling, wooden floors and timbers and is resplendent with stained glass windows. It has been described as 'one of Ludlow's greatest treasures'. For a while in its long history it was run as a hotel. After the death of Prince Arthur in 1502, his widow, Catherine of Aragon, is said to have stayed for a while at Castle Lodge. She later married Arthur's brother, Henry VIII. The building was then turned into a prison where criminals sentenced by the Council in the Marches were sent and who described it as 'a hell'. In 1580 it was rebuilt by Thomas Sackford, a Council official and a 'man of standing at the court of Elizabeth I', and the timbered top storey was added about 1600 by Robert Berry. The walls were once covered in plaster, which was removed in 1895. For many years in the 19th century it was run as a boarding and day school for young ladies.

At the turn of the century it was owned by Mr. W.E. Sharp, who also owned the **Angel Hotel** in Broad Street, and run by his wife, Phoebe Ellen. In 1926 it was described as a 'board house' run by a Mrs. E.P. Sharp and owned by Mr. Robert Kendrick Sharp, of the **Angel Hotel**.

By 1929 it was a 'private hotel' with 17 bedrooms, one bathroom and two toilets, with Mrs. P.E. Sharp as proprietoress. *Woolleys Ludlow Guide* of that year contains a quote from *The Queen* magazine: 'In Salop I can advise the little town of Ludlow, where write Mrs. Sharp, Castle Lodge (private hotel), an old-fashion oak panelled house, close to the castle, most moderate terms; cooking and attendance good; quite a unique place. Has given much satisfaction to *Queen* readers'. Mrs. Sharp died in 1934 and Castle Lodge was sold to Mr. Perry Brown, a journalist, for £1,500 in 1937. In 1946 Brown sold it for £7,000 to the brewers, Trouncer and Co., of Shrewsbury, who in turn sold it to the Westminster Bank for £7,750 in 1951. It was later used as offices by the Suez Canal company. In 1991 it was bought by Mr. and Mrs. W.T. Pearson, who began a programme of restoration and repair after which it was utilised in the television dramas of Moll Flanders and Tom Jones. Mrs. Pearson claims to have seen the ghost of Catherine of Aragon about seven years ago, always on a sunny summer's afternoon at 4 o'clock. The fortunes of **Castle Lodge** as a hotel are to be revived, with South Shropshire District Council having agreed the change of use.

When the front gate is shut after closing hours the only way of knowing that the **Rose and Crown** exists is by the sign hanging over Church Street, a narrow pedestrianised lane which up until the 1940s was still cobbled. But when the gate is open, a little gem of a pub is revealed. It nestles at the end of a courtyard with buildings on either

side and is part of a late 15th-century group including two shops adjoining the street (one survives at No. 5a). The three buildings occupied a plot 49½ft. wide, based on three times the standard medieval measurement of a pole or perch (16½ft.). The deeds for the inn go back as far as 1102 and there is still a remnant in a rear stone wall of a 13th-century two-light mullioned window with trefoil heads showing that the building may have been associated with the nearby College of Priests, or some other religious order. The inn's cellars are believed to have a passage leading to St. Laurence's church. At the time of the Reformation

*The sign for the **Rose and Crown** is above the gate that leads into this courtyard inn.*

there were supposed to be underground passages from the church to the castle and also to the **Exchange** and the **Bull**.

In the 15th century, drinks, including mulled beer with ginger, spice and brandy, would have been taken in front of an open log fire in the inn's kitchen, with a roast on the spit. Some evenings Travelling Players, all

*An advertisement for the **Rose and Crown** in the mid-1970s.*

male, would have come into the yard, and beer and wine would have overflowed. The whole place, including the balcony windows, would have been packed with onlookers all out to enjoy the show. The inn then had as many as 14 bedrooms and there was stabling for 20 horses and standing room for three more.

During the 17th century the **Rose and Crown** was owned by the Ludlow Corporation and leased to Ralph Goodwyn, a long-serving Ludlow M.P. and deputy secretary and clerk with the Council in the Marches, who sub-let the property at a considerable profit.

In the latter part of that century, Thomas Hill, described as a victualler, ran the pub and in 1686 he left a probate inventory valued at £25 10s., which, after deductions, came to £13 10s. The inn used to be one of the coaching houses for the Bewdley coaches when 'one for the road' was a protection against the cold of the journey over Clee Hill.

THE ROSE & CROWN
CHURCH STREET,
LUDLOW
Telephone: 0584 2098

16th Century

BAR SNACKS
COFFEE

Greenall Whitley Beers

In 1859 the landlord was Thomas Amis and in 1888 William Meredith. A return of licensed houses in Ludlow for 1901 showed that the **Rose and Crown** (a name which indicates loyalty to the monarch and to England) comprised a bar, two parlours, kitchen and six bedrooms. There was stabling for 14 horses. It was described as a market house and owned by Walter Thomas, of Old Street, Ludlow, and occupied by Walter Woodhouse. It had been leased to Ind Coope and Co. for 10 years from 1897 and by 1905 David Cumming Campbell was landlord. He was still there in 1926, but John Henry Morris was at the helm by 1941.

By 1955 it was owned by the Wrekin Brewery with Mr. R. (Mac) McHattie, a London Scot, as landlord. He had been in the licensing trade for 20 years, first at the **Bell**, then the **Nelson** before taking over the **Rose and Crown**. He was once an accountant with the Shell Oil Company in Venezuela. In 1992 the proprietors were Eric and Maureen Getting. As it moves into the 21st century there is still a medieval atmosphere about the inn, which boasts a large function room upstairs containing Victorian stained glass.

*The **Harp Inn**, now an Art Gallery, is at the end of Harp Lane.*

On a 700-year-old site at the end of the row of shops between Church Street and Harp Lane, stood the **Harp Inn** (James I was the first king to include it in the royal coat of arms). Before becoming a public house in the 17th century it had seen many uses including a butchers and barber surgeons. It was the third, possibly the fourth, **Harp** in Ludlow. In a directory of 1859, the licensee is given as Thomas Owen with the address as Harp Lane. Alternatively, in an 1868 directory the address is given as 1 Church Street. It closed as a licensed house in the 1870s and has been various shops ever since. For some years the upstairs part was used as the Ludlow Boy Scouts headquarters. Now it is an art gallery.

One of the best documented hostelries in Ludlow is the much altered **Church Inn** at The Butter Cross. Proudly on display in the bar is a list of the leaseholders and owners going back to 1439 when Richard Sibbeton was named. The inn stands on an ancient site, dating back to the 14th century at least, near the church of St. Laurence and was originally called the **Cross Keys**, a common sign in Christian heraldry referring to St. Peter to whom Jesus said 'I will give unto thee the keys of the Kingdom of Heaven'.

When the church tower was being built in 1470, there are records of expenditure on refreshments: 'Item in expencs of mete and drinke to wayn men [waggoners] carieng xx fother ston 2s 6 half'. There are also yearly entries of the cost of breakfasts and dinners at the making of the paschal candle—an immense taper which was lighted on Easter Eve and kept burning until Easter Day, in pre-Reformation times.

*The **Church Inn** is well hidden behind the Butter Cross.*

These expenses were succeeded in the 17th century by charges for regaling strange preachers, after their sermons, at the New House which stood in front of the **Cross Keys**.

The pub belonged to the Palmers' Guild, a brotherhood of leading burgesses formed in 1250, which engaged in educational, religious and charitable works. Palmer means pilgrim and pilgrims to the Holy Land carried palm branches. The Guild's original purpose was to support priests who would then intercede for the souls of living and dead members. It came to own a great deal of property in Ludlow, and members even came from other parts of the country.

In 1551 the pub was handed over to the Ludlow Corporation after the Dissolution which caused religious houses, including those belonging to the Palmers' Guild, to be surrendered. The Corporation continued to own it for the next 300 years, during which time it had several different uses including those of barber-surgeon, blacksmith and malster.

The *Universal British Directory* of 1790 shows it was still called the **Cross Keys** with John Aingel as innkeeper. In 1792 it became the **Wine Tavern near the Cross**, a medieval High Cross which stood in front of nearby Tamberlaine House (now an estate agents), that was replaced in 1743 by the Butter Cross, at a cost of £1,000, a handsome stone building used as a butter market. The upper floor housed the Blue Coat Charity School and from 1955 to 1974 it was the town's museum.

There is also a reference to a **Wine Vaults** near the Cross in 1791, but this may have been the same premises as it is definitely known by this name in the latter part of the 19th century. The reference came in an advert headed 'Ludlow, June 9th, 1791':

Wine Vaults and Brandy Warehouse (Late Farrer's)

John Thomas, Printer, Stationer, etc.
Respectfully acquaints the Publick that he has taken the House late
in the possession of Mr Joshua Farrer, near the Cross, and
purchased his stock of Wines and Spiritous Liquors, which are of
the first Quality, and which those who are pleased to favour him
with their orders may constantly be supplied with on the lowest
Terms, for ready Money. Their favours will always be attended to
with Punctuality and acknowledged with Gratitude.
Genteel Apartments to be Let,
with every necessary accommodation.
One hundred dozen of good Glass Bottles to be disposed of.
Joshua Farrer begs leave to recommend his Successor, Mr John
Thomas, to his Friends and Publick, being convinced that he is
enabled to serve them with wines and spirits of the best quality
and on the most reasonable Terms.

The church is only a stagger away and the pub would have been the first port of call for thirsty members of the congregation. At least one rector apparently had only himself to blame for his flock being led

*Once the **Wine Vaults** now the **Church Inn**.*

astray. An American tourist, Anna Maria Fay, on visiting Ludlow in the 1850s wrote to her mother: 'Mr Phillips, the rector, is a miserably low churchman—indeed they say he is a very bad man and his face justifies the report. He is so unpopular that the Dissenting Chapels and the alehouses are filled on Sundays'.

In 1848 the inn and several other properties was sold by the Corporation to help pay the costs of a law suit. Between 1865 and 1876 the building housed a druggist, one Ambrose Grounds, who was mayor of Ludlow in 1852/3. It reverted to the licensed trade, however, when John Wollaston bought the premises in 1876 and ran it as **Wollaston's Wine Vaults**.

His widow let the premises out for £85 a year in 1890 to a malster before selling it on in 1895 to the Cheltenham Original Brewery Company, who renamed it the **Exchange Vaults**, possibly after a stagecoach. By 1901 it was known as the **Wine Vaults** and owned by Ind Coope & Co. of Burton-on-Trent and occupied by Thomas Withnall. With a rateable value of £39 2s. 6d., it comprised a bar, smoke room, two parlours, office and 10 bedrooms. It remained under the ownership of Ind Coope until 1954 when it was sold to Mitchell & Butlers.

After an extensive refurbishment it became the **Gaiety Inn** in 1974, but it was renamed once again in 1979 as the **Church Inn**. An advert in that year proclaimed the **Church Inn**, Butter Cross, as a free house with the new proprietors, J.T. and M. Jones. The advert added: 'Accommodation (full fire certificate), Bar Meals, Restaurant, Morning coffee, Traditional ales. Game and Coarse fishing available'.

There were two more owners until, in April 2000, it was taken over and run by Mr. G. Willson-Lloyd, himself mayor of Ludlow in 1993-94.

CHAPTER FIVE

Upper Broad Street

Described by John Leland in 1540 as 'the fayrest part of the town'; in the 1790 *Universal British Directory* as 'an elegant structure of hewn stone'; and by Nicholas Pevsner in 1958 as 'one of the most memorable streets in England', Broad Street is wide and spacious and slopes southwards to the Teme with pavements raised by a cobbled incline. It was a part of Ludlow 'much resorted to by the inhabitants as an agreeable and genteel promenade'. Well-to-do people used to live there in elegant houses secure in the knowledge that the still present Broadgate, which used to be a toll gate and part of the 13th-century stone walls surrounding the town centre, was closed at night.

Being on the main highway to the south, the street was also recognised as one of the major areas for inns and taverns, with visitors bent on business at the castle, first with its royal inhabitants and then with the Council in the Marches. There were also the visitors to the fairs and to the many specialised markets held in different parts of the town, such as the beast market, the corn market, and the apple market. There was a constantly changing mixture of inns and alehouses to keep Broad Street 'the best accustomed street in the town'. As far back as 1626 the street could boast of no fewer than six of the 16 inns known by their signs at a time when a hundred Ludlow residents were allowed by law to sell beer or ale.

During the 18th and 19th centuries, the **Crown** and the **Angel**, facing each other across Broad Street at the Butter Cross end and near the town centre, had become the leading coaching inns.

From the Butter Cross, on the east side of Broad Street was first the **Swann Inn** (the badge of the Bohun family, one of whom married

1—Swann	8—Crown
2—Angel	9—Swan & Falcon
3—*Unnamed*	10—White Hart
4—Peacock	11—Royal Kent, Victoria & Crown
5—Star	12—Talbot
6—Anchor	13—Seven Stars
7—*Unnamed*	

*All the pubs described in this chapter
have ceased to trade*

The upper part of Broad Street.

Henry IV, and a sign also used by Henry VIII) at No. 5 in the late 16th to early 17th centuries.

The inn was mentioned in records dated 1541. It was later owned in 1669 by Mr. Gabriell Cadman, 'distiller of hott waters' by which time the **Swann** had become a butcher's shop and by 1841 a shoemaker's. Cadman himself was a brewer at No. 7. The three-storied building with bay windows on the upper floors is still used as two shops.

The earliest known reference to the **Angel** (houses of this name derived from the Annunciation of the Virgin) at 9 Broad Street is in 1551, though the building dates from before 1439 when merchants lived there. It was not always an inn or hotel, having been occupied by a bookseller and then a gunsmith in the mid-17th century. At one time the **Angel** was a two-storey building and the inn sign, denoting the early connection between religious establishments and travellers' hostels, swung from a post in the middle of the street. It was one of the inns which catered for officials, lawyers and litigants attending the Council in the Marches during its heyday between 1525 and 1642.

Landlords at the **Angel** were often men of means. Walter Langford, for example, paid 35s. in 1570 to lease 'one pewe next unto the church wedding doere' at St. Laurence's church, and Thomas Jones, owner and landlord from 1713 to 1731, was on the Corporation and on his death left possessions valued at £293 5s., of which £150 was for wine, beer, ale and cider. The **Angel** then had 18 rooms—of which 14 were bedrooms—and over 80 chairs.

After visiting Ludlow in 1784, John Byng, who was commissioned in the army, although belonging to the well known

*De Grey's Café was once part of the **Swann**.*

naval family, wrote: 'After teaing at our inn (**Angel**; very good) we walked about the town, admired the wideness and well building of the streets'. He then went to the theatre on the western side of Mill Street opposite the Grammar School. Byng stayed another night at the **Angel** leaving after having breakfasted 'upon buttermilk; which allways does me much good'.

Drunken brawls were commonplace in Ludlow, as in 1629 when two glovers had 'opprobrious words' in the **Angel** 'about a flagon of ale while they played at cards' resulting in 'many blows'. On a brighter note, travelling players from Hereford performed at the **Angel** in 1713. William Neve Junior was landlord of the **Angel** for 21 years from 1759.

In 1800 the owner, Mrs. Elizabeth Toldervy, added to the original premises part of the adjoining leasehold house which became a first-floor billiard room, with two stables and coach office on the ground floor. Later Henry Harding acquired part of Taylor's Yard at the back of the **Angel** and erected there a range of coach-houses and other buildings.

In 'Reminiscences of an old inhabitant (1809-30)', published in the *Ludlow Advertiser* of 1903, Mary Jones, who was then 93 and the town's oldest inhabitant, wrote:

> Mail coaches covered the distance [to London] in two days and I remember travelling about 80 years ago by the Aurora, leaving the **Angel** one Saturday afternoon, staying the night in Worcester, starting from there at 5 o'clock Sunday morning, through Oxford at midday when the colleges were coming out of church and passing Tyburn turnpike when the London bells were chiming for evening service.

*At the beginning of the 20th century the **Angel** was still rendered.*

Mary was the youngest of 11 children of Edward and Annie Collier, Edward being a gardener and licensee of the **King's Arms** where the family lived in what is now 41 Bull Ring.

On the Aurora's return journey from London, Mabbit, one of Ludlow's most famous coachmen, would blow his post horn when a mile distant on the Hereford Road. At the **Angel**, the domestics and ostlers would hear and go into action in preparation for the arrival of hungry and

*The upper end of Broad Street about 1916. The **Angel** has been stripped of its render to expose the splendid timberwork.*

54

thirsty passengers. A black and white house at this point is still named Mabbit's Horn.

In 1811 there were 19 departures from Broad Street each week and the same number of arrivals. Other mail coaches and posts left and returned to Broad Street daily, and with the additional private posting—vehicles which could be hired from Joseph Farrar at the **Angel** in 1782, who advertised 'neat post chaises, able horses and careful drivers'—the street must have been perpetually busy.

In an almanack of 1820, mail and stage coaches from the **Angel Inn** were listed as follows:

Royal Mail coach to Church Stretton, Shrewsbury, Chester, Manchester, Liverpool, Holy-head every Monday, Wednesday and Friday at 1 o'clock. Returns the following days (Saturday excepted) about the same hour.

The Shropshire Hero post coach, every Tuesday, Thursday and Saturday mornings at 12 o'clock.
Returns the following day about same hour.

To Leominster and Hereford:
The Union Post coach every Sunday, Tuesday and Thursday at 1 o'clock. Returns the following mornings about 12.
The Shropshire Hero Post Coach every Monday, Wednesday, and Friday at 1 o'clock. Returns the following mornings about 12.

The **Angel** was the last of the Ludlow inns to end such traffic after the arrival of the railway in 1852.

In 1802 Lord Nelson was given the Freedom of the Borough in a ceremony at the **Angel** in a room which came to be known as the 'Nelson Room'. Accompanied by his friends, Sir William and Lady Hamilton (Nelson's Emma), Nelson came in a coach pulled by teams of cheering citizens. He had been travelling in the Marches and Wales so that Sir William could inspect estates in Wales and Nelson could visit the Forest of Dean to see at first hand the quality of the oak to be used in the building of England's fighting ships. Afterwards he addressed the cheering crowd from one of the upstairs bow windows. A few years later Napoleon's brother, Lucien Bonaparte, King of Naples, was dined at the **Angel** after arriving in Ludlow as a prisoner of war and before commencing his stay at Dinham House, with his wife and extensive family, as a prisoner for six months.

TO COACH PROPRIETORS,
INNKEEPERS,
AND OTHERS IN THE POSTING LINE.

TO BE SOLD BY

AUCTION,

BY T. GRIFFITHS,

(By Order of the Assignees, of WILLIAM WHITNEY, late of LUDLOW, in the County of SALOP, Innkeeper, a Bankrupt,)

On **MONDAY**, the 4th of **FEBRUARY, 1822,**

AND FOLLOWING DAYS, UNTIL THE WHOLE IS DISPOSED OF,

At the ANGEL-INN, in LUDLOW,

AFORESAID,

ALL THE

Household Goods
AND
FURNITURE,

PLATE, GLASS, LINEN, CHINA,

WINES, SPIRITUOUS LIQUORS,
HORSES,

Coaches, Chaises, Harness, and other Effects.

*Sale of the effects of William Whitney, the bankrupt landlord of the **Angel Inn**.*

56

After the Napoleonic Wars, the changed economic circumstances resulted in a number of bankruptcies in the Broad Street area including that of William Whitney, the owner and landlord of the **Angel**, in 1821. The **Angel** was put up for auction. A note attached to the poster read:

> The **Angel Inn** is to be sold or let with immediate Possession.
> For particulars apply to Mr Henry Harding, Corve Street.

A week later there was another sale at the inn conducted again by T. Griffiths when items included '25 Post horses, 3 chaises, 2 stage coaches, several sets of harness, and various other articles'.

Three years later the **Angel** was back on the market again and described as:

> All that neat and very desirable Freehold Messuage, discharged of land tax, with the garden, offices, brewhouse, laundry, coach-house, stables and appurtenances thereto adjoining, most eligibly situated in Broad Street, and late in the occupation of Mr. Foxton.
> The premises consist of a very substantial brick-built messuage, replete with every convenience, and in good repair, having on the basement floor an entrance hall, two parlours, a large kitchen, housekeeper's room, butler's pantry, larder and good cellaring; on the first floor, two good airy bed-chambers, with a dressing room, and two other excellent bedrooms, with closets; on the second floor, six comfortable lodging rooms, and a store room.
> N.B. A small part of the Garden is held by lease under the Corporation of Ludlow for a term of 31 years, under the yearly rent of one pound, one shilling.

After these sales, the inn continued to play a pivotal role in the town's affairs. Apart from its posting business it hosted a variety of functions including meetings of the local Lodge of Freemasons and the Conservatives. Soon after the Reform Act of 1832 an 'Ode on the **Angel**' was published. The first verse went:

> All who have good appetites, and for a dinner look,
> Should just step in the **Angel Inn**, and speak to Mrs Cook;
> On Friday night, there was a sight, to cheer each loyal soul,
> A hundred gallant Tories then, were seated round the bowl,
> Like gallant Cavaliers of the olden days.

The ode concluded:

> The spark is lit, Conservatives, let's blow it in a flame,
> And in the Club, each loyal hand, should now subscribe his name:
> And when in after time folks ask, where did this Club begin?
> Why at that famous dinner sure, held at the **Angel Inn**!
> By the gallant Cavaliers of the olden time.

By 1840 the **Angel** was being called a hotel, a term originating in London and coming to mean a high class inn—yet in the same year the establishment was the scene of a violent incident. On 20 August came an unwelcome visitor—one Josiah Misters, aged 23 or 24, of sallow complexion and short black hair, the son of an Excise officer stationed at Leominster. He had been tracking from fair to fair a Mr. Ludlow, a corn dealer and butcher from Birmingham who carried a large sum of money in gold on his person. Mr. William Ludlow came to Ludlow and booked in at the **Angel Hotel**. Misters pretended to the chambermaid that he was a friend of Ludlow and was also given a room. However, by some mistake the room assigned to Ludlow was actually slept in by another person—William Mackreth, a commercial traveller for a Bristol firm—and Ludlow slept in a different room.

At four o'clock the next morning Mackreth woke to a hand over his face and the cut of an open razor. He jumped out of bed shouting, 'Help! Murder! Fire!' and the assailant fled. With throat cut and his face slashed 'across his mouth literally from ear to ear', he was unable to speak when help arrived, but managed to write 'I have been

Misters.

murdered by a villain'. Drops of blood from the razor led to Misters' room where a large blood stain on one of the curtains was found. The blood-stained razor was later found in a yard below Misters' bedroom window. Misters was arrested and charged with attempted murder at Ludlow Court where Mackreth, having recovered, gave evidence. He

Mackreth.

58

was committed for trial at Shrewsbury Assizes and six months later was found guilty and sentenced to be hanged. Despite his protestations of innocence, he was hanged in Shrewsbury, the last man in England to be hanged for attempted murder.

A few days later, the chambermaid at the **Angel** ran screaming downstairs that she had seen Misters walking in the passage. Other guests spoke of the little dark man who never appeared at breakfast. The practice of looking under the bed before retiring was indulged in by the people of Ludlow and continued for a long time.

In the early 1860s, Robert Edwards, a 35-year-old professional innkeeper from Chirk, became tenant of the **Angel**, then owned by the Rev. P.B. Adams, of Hopesay. The **Angel** flourished and was even honoured with a visit by the Prince of Wales in 1861. By 1870 Edwards had bought the **Feathers** but at first installed a manageress, Mrs. Wigley, and continued to live at the **Angel**. It was as landlord of the **Angel** that Edwards, who had been elected to the Borough Council in 1866, was made mayor of Ludlow in 1871 and re-elected in 1872.

In October 1876 an advertisement appeared in the *Ludlow Advertiser* on behalf of the **Angel** Hotel Company:

> The **Angel** Hotel, being for sale, and the present Tenant's lease expiring at Lady-Day, 1877, it is considered a fitting opportunity to attempt to provide an increased hotel accommodation which shall meet the requirements of the charming neighbourhood. Capital £8,000, in 800 shares of £10 each.

The **Angel** was bought in 1877 by a specially created company. In *Kelly's Directory* of 1900 an advert declared that the **Angel** was a 'First class family and commercial hotel and posting house (Mrs. W.H. Millward, proprietress), Omnibus meets all trains'. In 1901 it was owned by Mr. W.E. Sharp, of Castle House, Ludlow and occupied by Montague Kemp who was also a local councillor for Broad Street Ward. Described as a commercial and posting hotel, it comprised a bar, two parlours, commercial and coffee room, billiard room and 18 bedrooms. There was stabling, in good repair and clean, for 11 horses.

In 1909, with the advent of the motor car and when the proprietor was E.W. Bodenham, another advert for the **Angel** is of particular interest. Under the heading 'Posting' it read: 'Rubber tyred landaus, smart private broughams. Single horse vehicles 1s. per mile. Pair of horses 1s. 6d. per mile. Comfortable and reliable 4-seater motor car for hire by day or week'.

During the Second World War the **Angel** was taken over as an Army headquarters for the district and housed one of the well-known British Restaurants. After the fall of France some French naval officers were billeted there including the Count of Toulouse, former

*An early 20th-century advertisement for the **Angel Hotel**.*

commander of the *Sirocco*, which had taken part in Dunkirk, and an old Vice-Admiral.

After the war, the inn was bought by Southams Brewery, but was sold a few years later to a brewery from Liverpool, and sold again, in 1970, to Whitbreads. In 1951 it had suffered a 'modernisation' during which many features of antiquity were destroyed, leaving little apart from the 17th-century façade. The hotel stopped trading in the early 1990s and, after remaining empty for several years, has found a new lease of life as a centre for antiques and works of art. The old coaching stables and the Nelson room have been converted into shops and flats.

One of the earliest inns was probably at 10 Broad Street, next to the **Angel**, although its name is not known. Behind the present frontage, with its

*The **Angel** in 1999.*

60

Roundabout Stationery shop, is an eight-bay medieval range built in 1431-39, and overlooking a courtyard. Each bay is thought to have contained a chamber above with a stable below and used by the more wealthy travellers. There was probably a front range parallel to the

*No. 22 Broad Street, once the **Peacock Inn**.*

street, similar to the one at the **Bull**. It was owned by the Palmers' Guild with John Bengemyn as leaseholder. When the Palmers' Guild ceased to function the building was owned for many years by Ludlow Corporation.

On the corner of Brand Lane at 22 Broad Street, now a video emporium, was the **Peacock** tavern (providing great scope for the sign-painters) in the 18th century. A painting by Samuel Scott in about 1766 shows the **Peacock**, then kept by a William Haycock, with a prominent sign board. On the other side of the road is another inn, the **Seven Stars** (see below). In 1790 the innkeeper of the **Peacock** was Mrs. Wall.

*Nos. 24-25 Broad Street, once the **Star Inn**.*

At Nos. 24-25, now two houses, in the 17th century was the **Star Inn** (originally denoting the Star of Bethlehem but after 1634 a 16-pointed star appeared in the arms of the Worshipful Company of Innholders). Simon Bradshaw (died 1638) owned the inn which was tenanted by Edward Miles, a carrier during the Civil War.

Further down at Nos. 28-30 was the **Anchor** or **Anker** (probably referring to a symbolic meaning such as a 'steadfast anchor of the soul', although an 'Anker' is an old liquid measurement of approximately 8½ imperial gallons). The tenant, Mr. Thomas Edwards, was referred to as 'innholder' in 1610; it was run by the Bishops from 1648 to 1673. Both the **Star** and **Anchor** were of some repute as they were both included in the list of 16 inns known by their sign in 1626.

On the west side of Broad Street, No. 59 may have been a licensed premises in the 17th century. At any rate a William Willmott lived there and for his probate inventory, valued at £21 2s. 11d., he was described as an innkeeper and glover. Certainly next door at Nos. 56-58, and opposite the **Angel**, was the largest and at one time the most important inn in Ludlow—the **Crown**. Based on what was formerly two shops, it is first mentioned in 1504. In 1553 it was owned by William Foxe.

Mention of the inn occurred in 1603 when an informer recommended to the government an investigation into a meeting at the Sign of the **Crown**, to which Robert Townshend, a Catholic, had sent his servant to meet William Watson, a wanted Jesuit. During the Civil War (1642-51), Ludlow remained devoutly in support of Charles I and was one of the last places to surrender to Parliament. Thus it is likely that the sign, denoting loyalty to the reigning monarch, proudly swung until the end. If it came down during the Commonwealth it would doubtless have been put up again following the Restoration.

Richard Scott was the innkeeper in 1667 with six servants, and in 1672 the hearth tax showed it had 18 hearths, more than any other Ludlow house. An inventory in 1685 valued Scott's goods at £212 6s. 8d. There were 15 principal rooms including a dining room, great parlour, lower parlour and a number of named chambers, 11 of them containing beds, and among the items of furniture were 23 tables, 65 chairs and 230 pounds of pewter. Outside was a barn and mill-house. In addition to the usual range of functions held at inns, by 1685 the **Crown** could also boast a Judge's chamber.

The landlord in 1721 was John Mason, who stayed there until his death. He had previously been at the **Feathers** for three years. Another landlord, Thomas Jones, who died in 1731, kept nine casks of wine worth £90.

Over the years the **Crown** came to be one of the town's leading coaching inns. By 4 a.m. twice a week it would be alive to the clatter of horses' hoofs on the road, the crack of a coachman's whip and the sound of a post horn, with the departure of the Leek post coach on its 91 mile run to the seaside at Aberystwyth, which it reached in the evening. Two hours later the mail coach left for Worcester, where it met the London mail, the passengers reaching their destination early next morning, having supped at Oxford at 11 o'clock.

Sometimes a mishap occurred as in December 1788 when a large ladies' trunk went missing from behind a chaise somewhere between Ludlow and Newtown. A reward of five guineas was offered for information to be given to Mr. Williams, of the **Crown**. The long list of ladies' garments and sundry items it contained included '14 shifts, 16 pairs of silk stockings, 10 muslin nightcaps, 12 cambrick handkerchiefs, eight dimity petticoats, two dimity dressing gowns, six muslin and dimity gowns, a handsome black silk cloak trimmed with lace, and five pairs of shoes'.

In 1820 a Royal Mail coach was leaving the **Crown** for Worcester and London every Sunday, Tuesday, Wednesday, Friday and Saturday mornings at 6 o'clock (except Tuesday which morning it left at 5.30). The coach returned the same evening about 6. By this coach the London and other bags were either forwarded or brought the same day.

The **Crown** was also used by the townspeople for prestigious events. For instance, in 1788, a special dinner costing 2s. 6d. was held there to commemorate the centennial of the 'Glorious Revolution', which saw the overthrow of James II and the establishment of his daughter Mary and her husband William of Orange to the throne. Thomas Knight, Esq., took the chair, supported on either side by the Members for the Borough: Edward, Lord Clive and Richard Payne Knight. A report of the occasion stated:

> To the glorious and immortal memory of King William, the Promoter and firm Supporter of our present Constitution, a very fine painting of King William, the property of Mr George Payne, was brought into the room, and held up to the company whilst the toast was drunk with three cheers; the Portrait was afterwards presented to the Corporation, who ordered the same to be placed in some conspicuous part of the Town Hall, and the next glass was filled up to the Donor, with the cheer of three times three.

A hundred years later a letter appeared in the *Ludlow Advertiser*. It read:

In 1888 I was turned out of my comfortable quarters and found myself in a druggists' warehouse, redolent of fly powder and sheep dip. After 12 months of misery and disgust I was looking forward to another revolution which would again land me in the serene atmosphere of the Council Chamber. But judge of my distress when I find that I 'of glorious and immortal memory' am to be relegated to the backstairs of that building erected in commemoration of the benefits received under monarchial government ... My friend and former owner, Mr. Payne, who presented me to the town, would be pained.

The painting of William III.

The letter, signed William III, seemed to do the trick as the painting was eventually rehung in the Council Chamber. When the Town Hall was demolished in 1986, the painting again went into storage, and now has a temporary home in the reception area of Ludlow Town Council at the Butter Cross. Opposite is a portrait of Oliver Cromwell!

In 1794 'the Nobility, gentlemen, travellers and others' of Ludlow were informed by Richard Hodnett 'that he succeeds Mr. Williams as Master of the **Crown Inn** at Christmas next in which capacity his utmost attention and diligence will be exerted to provide every accommodation which is generally expected in a large, commodious and old established inn'. Hodnett assured 'the Publick, that the united Endeavours of himself and those employed under him will at all Times be used to deserve their Patronage, and that he shall trust more to his future conduct, than to a long Parade of Professions, to secure his Claim to Encouragement and Approbation'. His

Stage Coach Cottage.

predecessor had occupied the **Crown** for 30 years.

After the Napoleonic wars, the proprietor, then William Green, was faced with financial problems forcing him to sell up and move his sign further down the road in 1818. After the sale, the building was divided into two once again with No. 56 becoming a chemist's and No. 58 a manufacturer of hats. Later it became a Gas Show Room and more recently it housed part of Choices and a balti house. The only indication of its once proud role is a cottage—a former stable at the rear of No. 56— called the 'Stage Coach'.

*Nos. 56-58 Broad St., once the **Crown**.*

The next two properties have also been licenced houses in the past. The **Swan and Falcon** (emblems which were respectively connected to Henry IV and the duke of York) was at No. 55 in the 17th and 18th centuries. Thomas Michell was innholder at the end of the 17th century and in 1694 left a probate inventory valued at £161. It was mentioned in a list of licensed inns in 1742. It is now part of Choices, a video shop.

*The **Swan and Falcon** in 2002.*

Adjoining was another 18th-century tavern—the **White Hart** (a badge dating back to Richard II's heraldic symbol)—at No. 54. In 1667 the head of house was Thomas Michell, a victualler. The property was rebuilt in 1771 and is now a mature Georgian house of three stories used by the Ludlow Division of the Conservative Association.

William Green continued to trade under the sign of the **Crown** at No. 52. There had been another inn on this site, which is mentioned in records for 1550 and 1553. It was then called the **Falcon** (the personal badge of Richard, duke of York, 1411-1460, manorial lord of Ludlow and owner of the castle, and a reminder that for centuries falconry was a royal sport), when it was owned by the heirs of Richard Whittall. It was also mentioned in 1626 as being one of only 16 inns known by its sign although recognisances to sell beer or ale had been granted to 100 Ludlow residents. In 1743-46 it was rebuilt for Richard Salwey to a design by William Baker. It was a large residential mansion of early Georgian design with a fine brick front. Later it became the home of Sir Charles Knowles, who used to turn out in a carriage and four, and it was on his death that it reverted to being an inn.

Auctions were held there including one in January 1826, of '124 capital oak timber trees of large dimensions fit for the Navy'. They came from a farm called Stocking in Stanton Lacy. The new **Crown** must have been a prestigious inn, for in 1832 it received royal patronage by a 13-year-old Victoria—in five years time to become Queen—and her mother, the duchess of Kent, who were staying at nearby Oakly Park. In their honour it was grandly re-named **Royal Kent, Victoria and Crown Hotel.**

In 1843 it was owned and run by Green's widow, Elizabeth, described as being 'portly, middle-aged and bustling, who was aided in her business by her son, and quite a bevy of darling daughters, whose beauty was something more than a mere local fancy'. Even so, it closed in 1848 to become a family residence for Captain Adrian Jones. Then, in 1879, it was replaced by a Wesleyan Chapel, which still opens its doors to worshippers today.

Three doors down at No. 49 is the grand looking Oriel House, named from the oriel window high up on the Bell Lane side, which it abuts. It used to be the **Talbot** Inn, first referred to in 1492 and named after the Talbots—the earls of Shrewsbury—who had owned the site from before 1439 until about 1481. The sign would have shown a Talbot—a white hunting dog with black spots similar to the modern Dalmatian—which appeared on the

*Oriel House, once the **Talbot**.*

coat of arms of the earls. In 1553 the owner was John Bradshaw with John Alsop as the tenant.

After 1600 it was known alternatively as the **Antyloppe** (an antelope with chain and collar is featured in one of the misericords in the parish church, and was the emblem used by Henry VI; it was also used by the duke of Gloucester) or the **Rayndeer** (with the antlers making for a distinctive sign) until the 1660s, when it closed down. It was rebuilt as a house in 1669 for a Mr. William Dawes. It might also have been known as the **Greyhound**, for such an inn is recorded in this vicinity. During the 17th-century Civil War the **Greyhound** billeted soldiers.

Further down at No. 38 in the mid-18th century was the **Seven Stars** (an often quoted astrological sign of the Middle Ages and usually shown as the seven stars of the Bear constellation) which in its earlier life was a rectory. Innholder Edward Keysale left a probate inventory in 1743 valued at £18 5s. 6d. A later innkeeper, called John Dean,

The Georgian mansion that replaced the **Seven Stars**.

developed Dean's Yard at the back of the **Seven Stars**. The Easter Rate Book of 1766 showed the innkeeper was John Thomas, who was married, whilst the property had a window tax (which replaced the hearth tax) of 1s. 4d. There is a painting by Samuel Scott in about 1766 showing Mr. Thomas and his wife outside the inn, which is painted white and faced the **Peacock**, across the street. Two years later it was replaced by the five-bay Georgian mansion which still occupies the site. The artist lived for three years at No. 35, on the corner with Silk Mill Lane.

CHAPTER SIX

Lower Broad Street & Ludford

Below the 13th-century Broad Gate, the sole survivor of seven such gates which once guarded the whole town, is Lower Broad Street, which stretches sharply down to the old packhorse bridge spanning the Teme. With the wool and cloth industry prominent in Ludlow's early history, there were at one time no fewer than 11 mills along the river including several fulling mills. Spinning and weaving was often done on a domestic basis and many of the residences in Lower Broad Street were weavers' cottages. Nestling by Broad Gate, topped by a 17th-century house, is the **Wheatsheaf** Inn, the sole survivor of nine pubs in that area.

There was an inn on this site in the 16th century and possibly earlier. Its reputation was then not of the highest as a Ludlow court record of 1600 suggests. The innkeepers, Ellis and Mary Darby, were

*The **Wheatsheaf** and Broad Gate in the 1920s.*

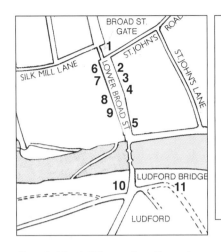

1—Wheatsheaf *	
2—Barley Mow	
3—Paul Pry	
4—Crown & Horseshoes	
5—Bell	
6—Mermaid	
7—Vineyard	
8—Dial	
9—Old Stag's Head	
10—Charlton Arms *	
11—Old Bell	
*—*Open in 2002*	

Lower Broad Street.

fined 40 shillings for 'keeping an ale house in Broad Street below the gate, without a licence, and at all hours of the day and night time, harboured in their house divers lewd and evil disposed persons, rogues, vagabonds, minstrels, pedlars, tinkers, beggars and such like, drinking, bowling, carousing and playing at unlawful games as well for money as for ale'.

The present **Wheatsheaf** (one of the devices on the arms of the Brewers' Company) was rebuilt across the town ditch—it actually straddles the ditch—after most of the properties leading from the gate to the river were razed by the town's Royalist defenders to clear a field of fire during the Civil War. After the hostilities, priority was given to replacing houses damaged during the war, with Corporation properties being given incentives for quick re-building. The **Wheatsheaf** site was leased to Thomas Price in 1655 with the 'condition to build', but nine years later the lease was re-issued to William Woodall, a carpenter, on similar terms and work was not finished until 1668.

In the 1780s the **Wheatsheaf** was a corporation leasehold, with 'a room or cellar commonly called the dungeon' under Broad Gate House kitchen. With the inn were associated a barn or beasthouse below Old Street Gate, sublet to nailers in 1788, and by 1806 converted into three dwellings. In 1855 a garden in Frog Lane (now St. John's Lane) with a blacksmith's shop and stables were added to the **Wheatsheaf** tenancy and part of the town ditch was used as a garden from 1841. The inn was enfranchised by the Corporation in 1850 and the Frog Lane property in 1855. The complex of cellars and wine vaults underneath the pub, together with the bricked-up openings of passages, fuelled the stories of secret underground passages to the castle which were used by carousing soldiers or by a priest after saying mass—forbidden after the Reformation. Ghost stories naturally exist including one of a lady-in-waiting and a child, and another of a man who may be one of the 'rogues, vagabonds, beggars and such like' who used this inn in the past.

In a 1790s directory, the **Wheatsheaf** was listed with James Mantle as innkeeper; in 1859 the innkeeper was Edward Morris. In 1900 it was owned and occupied by Henry Rogers. At that time the property, with a rateable value of £26, comprised a bar, parlour, kitchen and five bedrooms with stabling, on the other side of the road at the front, for three horses. Its trade was mainly of an agricultural nature. Rogers was still there in 1926. In 1941 it was still in the same family, being run by his widow, Mrs. Jane Rogers.

The **Wheatsheaf** was always known for its 'home brew'd ales' and it was the last pub in the town to brew its own beer, doing so until the Second World War when a man called Corbett was the licensee. The exterior of the building is still distinguished by a Gothic ogee-headed window. The ogee, consisting of two curves each drawn from one centre and meeting in a point at the top, was introduced about 1300 and was

*The **Wheatsheaf** in the 1950s, still advertising its home-brewed beers.*

THE WHEATSHEAF INN

BUILT
INTO
THE
TOWN
WALL

Good
Food
Guide
1976.
Egon
Ronay
Book
of
Good
Pubs

LUDLOW'S OLDEST AND MOST PICTURESQUE INN
Adjoining the only gate to the town
Telephone: **LUDLOW 2980**

*A mid-1970s advertisement for
the* **Wheatsheaf**.

especially popular in the 14th century.

In 1950, when structural alterations were carried out, a 'Tick' book was found at the back of an old cupboard in the inn by Andrew Robertson, the licensee. The long and very narrow book had been kept by a predecessor in the 1850s when, apparently, it was the custom for practically everyone, from affluent farmer to farm worker, to have current 'tick' accounts at their local inns. From the evidence of this book, everyone paid up. There is a record of a farmer and his wife staying the night at the inn. Bed and Breakfast for two was 2s., with breakfast consisting of home-cured ham and eggs. But the farmer did not settle the bill until the following month. Other items bought on 'tick' were 1oz. of tobacco for 1d., 2 pints of ale for 6d., and half a pint of gin for 10d. One of the contra accounts was for 50 gallons of ale (1s. 6d.) for 'old Childe and self' at £3 15s. A chandler's cottage nearest the Gate has since been incorportated into the inn.

The **Wheatsheaf** *in 2001.*

On the east side of Lower Broad Street at No. 16 was the **Barley Mow** (a barley stack was one of the earliest signs used to indicate that beer was sold on the premises). It was rebuilt in 1620 and survived the razing of buildings during the

Civil War. In the 1660s Edmund Dillow, a victualler, lived there. The last man in Ludlow to wear a perugue, or periwig for fashion's sake was an innkeeper at the **Barley Mow** in the 1770s or 1780s. In 1790 it was run by Mrs. Harding and is mentioned in a list of the town's inns in 1792. It was owned by the Corporation in 1843, and leased to the executors of Thomas Cook, mason, at a rent of 8s. The head of house was Thomas Jukes, a joiner with six children. In 1859 the innkeeper was William Cook.

The inn was heavily restored during the Victorian period including the use of green glazed tiles below the bow windows. In 1888 the **Barley Mow** was run by Benjamin Jukes, described as a 'licenced victualler, brewer, joiner, etc'. In 1897 the landlord seems to have run foul of the law for he was fined 10s. with 18s. costs for supplying drink to a drunken person and, having not changed his habits, was soon after fined 20s. with 15s. costs for permitting drunkenness. After several changes, by 1900 the inn was run by John Sheldon rapidly followed in 1901 by Charles Bywater, when it was owned by Eley's Stafford Brewery Co. It then consisted of a bar, kitchen, sitting room and six bedrooms described as being in good repair and clean.

More recently, the **Barley Mow** had a close association with the Ludlow and District Licensed Victuallers' Association. Landlord Reginald Banks was secretary in the 1920s and '30s; a position taken up by his widow, Elizabeth, in 1941. Mrs. Banks was also President for a couple of years and spent over 40 years in the licensed trade. It remained a public house until 1964, when a brewery change of ownership caused closure. The building was allowed to fall into 'a sad state of total disrepair and was near to

*A new building on the site of the **Barley Mow**.*

collapse'. Eventually the District Council made a Compulsary Purchase Order enabling them to buy the property. A new three-storey private residence with bay windows now stands on the site.

At No. 21/22 was the **Paul Pry** inn, which may previously have been known as the **Nag's Head** (the original sign probably indicating that a horse could be had for hire) mentioned in a list of inns in 1792 and which stood on a 13th-century site. It was given its new name in 1842 following the popularity of a play of that name written by John Poole in 1825 about a man who introduced himself with 'I hope I don't intrude' yet was always meddling in other people's affairs. Inn signs typically show a man listening at a door marked 'private'. In 1841 the inn was owned by a Mrs. Stephens with William Cook as innkeeper. He was married and had two servants. The pub closed in the 1870s and is now two houses.

*The **Paul Pry** is now two houses.*

The sign of the **Crown & Horseshoes** (indicating loyalty to the monarch and good luck or protection against witches) at No. 23 was recorded in 1742 in a list of licensed inns and in a local directory of 1822. In 1841 it was owned by the executors of John Harley, dyer, and run by George Green, who was married with two children and had one servant. In 1868 it was called the **Crown and Three Horseshoes** (the latter probably referring to the Worshipful Company of Farriers) with Thomas Sheldon as innkeeper. Appropriately he was also described as a blacksmith. Then, after trading for well over a century, the inn closed down in 1878 when eight 'messuages' were built behind the property. It is now a private house.

*The **Crown and Horseshoes** is now a private house.*

The **Bell Inn** once stood at what is now part of St. John's House on the corner of Temeside. From the roof protruded a huge bell with below it a sign reading: 'R. A. Challoner. Good stabling'. It was, however, probably frequented by the poorer type of visitor to Ludlow and never enjoyed the prestige of its more illustrious predecessor as a coaching inn in Ludford.

The **Bell** sign had been transferred to Lower Broad Street following the closure of the inn in Ludford sometime in the mid-1820s. Parts of the former building date back to the 13th century when the Hospital of St. John was built on the site. A 13th-century archway was discovered when the front part of the house was removed for road widening in the 19th century. In 1843 it was owned by Edward Collerick with James Pillinger as the innkeeper. In 1888 the inn was run by William Russell,

*The **Bell** with Challoner as landlord.*

75

who was described as a 'licensed victualler, brewer and timber haulier'.

Eventually, the inn fell foul of the law. There had been disorderly conduct there under two licensees and three of its five entrances were shut down to make police control easier. But, in 1896, the local magistrates refused to renew its licence. This may have been part of a plan to reduce the number of public houses in the town.

On the west side of Lower Broad Street at No. 68 was the **Mermaid**, which traded in the late 17th and early 18th centuries. Is it incidential that a mermaid is featured in the St. Laurence misericords, symbolising a seductress luring men from the path of salvation? Was it named after the famous Mermaid Tavern in Bread Street, Cheapside, the famous meeting place of the wits, literary men and men about town in the early 17th century? Perhaps not, for by 1841 the building was a labourer's cottage and now it is a private residence.

The **Vineyard** is thought to have been a tavern at No. 63, for in December, 1822, a notice stated: 'To be let that excellent piece of garden ground called the Vine Yard, planted with choice fruit trees'. In the past the Vine was a

*Once the **Mermaid Inn**.*

*The **Dial** is now a charming cottage.*

common pub name and it was also a heraldic reference to the Worshipful Company of Distillers.

There was another 18th-century tavern, the **Dial** (usually indicating a nearby public clock), at Nos. 49/50. It must have been of some importance as it was among a list of licensed inns in 1747 and again in 1754. Even earlier, in 1667, it was occupied by George Castle, a victualler who was married with six children. Today it is a charming cottage with two bay windows.

The **Old Stag's Head** (a reference to stag hunting, a favourite royal sport) was at Nos. 37/39, operating again in the 18th century. It is also believed to be the site of the 13th-century **Robert Dul's tavern**, (probably the innkeeper's name) where in 1271 Thomas Gyllur knifed Elias Spark, of Onibury, during a drunken brawl.

*The **Old Stag's Head** in 2002.*

Crossing the Teme on the south side of Ludford Bridge, which used to link Shropshire with Herefordshire and dates back to at least the 15th century, stands the **Charlton Arms Hotel**, named after the Charltons, who were squires at Ludford from the mid-17th to the mid-19th century. It may originally have been called the **Red Lion** (originating from the badge of John of Gaunt, later duke of Lancaster, in the 14th century) and did not acquire its present name until about 1823. Sir Job Charlton was Speaker of the House of Commons and entertained James II at Ludford House near the church where Charlton is buried.

The hotel would have offered an excellent vantage point to witness the highlight of an annual procession during Rogation Days

*The **Charlton Arms** and the bridge over the river Teme about 1905.*

which combined both pagan and religious rites. On 'Processioning Day', boys from the various schools, accompanied by a clergyman, perambulated the boundaries of the town. Starting from St. Laurence's church, the boys, armed with birch boughs closely tied up, came to Ludford Bridge, where a decorated birch bough had been fixed. A 'tremendous fight for the possession of the bough upon the bridge,

*The **Charlton Arms** in the 1930s.*

78

took place between the different schools. This ended, the party marched to the Guildhall, to finish their work with a feast of plum buns'.

In 1875 it is recorded that the **Red Lion** or **Charlton Arms**, Ludford, together with Nos. 132 and 133 Tower Street, and a cottage in Burford, was settled on marriage of Emma Cantrell with Samuel Faulconbridge. In 1885 the landlord was John William Beaman. Petty Sessional records of 1896 show that the hotel was then owned by the Lichfield Brewery and that it consisted of a bar, kitchen, smoke-room and eight bedrooms and had stabling for 15 horses. It was run by George Wagstaffe who paid rates of

Recent advice from the ***Charlton Arms.***

£8. The nature of its trade was described as being 'agriculture and roadside'. The nearest public house was 50 yards away and there was a constables' station three-quarters of a mile distant, which meant its position was 'good' for police control. Its full licence had been granted in 1846. The hotel was run by a Susannah Martha Barnett in 1900.

A hotel brochure, printed sometime between the two world wars, read: 'It stands practically on the banks of the River Teme, near the natural weir and picturesque bridge which is the only approach to the town itself, and in consequence an ideal centre for the visitor'. Recent alterations to the hotel offer 'the most modern conveniences' and included the construction of 'a Dance Hall where dances were frequently held'. 'There is also extensive garage accommodation and nearby an up-to-date motor

The ***Charlton Arms*** *in 2001.*

*The **Charlton Arms** still stands guard over the river bridge.*

engineering works (Temeside Garage Ltd.) where repairs can be executed and cars hired.' Temeside Garage, now Ludford Bridge Services, were official repairers to the AA and RAC and were members of the H.F. Salvage Corps and offered 'towing, ambulance and lifting crane for breakdowns'.

The brochure continued: 'Special attention is given to the important matter of Cuisine', and added, 'although the best food is provided, the terms are most moderate as can be seen from the Tariff'. This showed that luncheon, hot was 3s. 6d., luncheon, cold 2s. 6d., with tea priced at 1s. 6d. and dinner at 5s. Inclusive boarding terms were from four guineas a week, a single room from 5s., a double room from 8s. and bed and breakfast 8s. 6d. a night. Extras included a bath and garage both at 1s. Ludlow was described as 'a sportsman's paradise' with splendid fishing in, and delightful boating on, the Teme; two meetings a year on the Bromfield race course, with an excellent golf course adjoining; together with bowls, cricket, football, hockey and swimming all catered for.

From about 1926 to 1941 the hotel was under the control of Charles Jubilee Harris. About 20 to 30 years ago the dance floor was abandoned and is now part of the rear car park.

In 1954 the **Charlton Arms** was apparently in danger of being closed down, an order for the closing of the premises having been made. But a week before the doors were to be finally closed Mr. H.A. Marler, licensee of the **Compasses Inn**, Corve Street, dropped in for a drink. He heard of the impending closure and within days he and his brother, Mr. W. Marler, bought it. Rumour was rife that the foundations of the building had been undermined by the Teme, but there was little substance to this as the inn is built on rock. It was then run as a free house by Mr. W. Marler.

In the village of Ludford stands a very distinguished private residence called the Old Bell House. It is a black-and-white, half-timbered country house, that makes use of mellow brick and includes several impressive chimney stacks, which was once a renowned coaching inn. It probably dates from about 1500 although the records only go back to 1614. In those early days it was a small inn called the **Three Crowns** (named after the three wise men and later referring to James I—the first monarch to rule over England, Scotland and Wales). This name did not appear in a document until 1773 when the lease was transferred to one Edward Carrier, a tailor of Ludlow. The house was

*The **Old Bell** in 2001.*

then described as 'formerly called the **Three Crowns** and now known as the sign of the **Bell**'. At that time the inn stood alongside the main road leading south, but in the early 19th century the road was diverted to the west, leaving this part of Ludford isolated on a *cul-de-sac*. Perhaps this was the reason that by 1828 the **Bell** had transferred to Lower Broad Street.

The **Old Bell** was transformed after the property was acquired by Mr. John Stallybrass at the beginning of the last century. Today the house is renowned for the oak panelling in the lounge, hall, study and dining room, and a wonderful plaster ceiling in the main bedroom. There is also a heated swimming pool in the ornate gardens.

CHAPTER SEVEN

The Bull Ring

Specialised markets took place in different parts of Ludlow of which the beast market, probably the 'largest, noisiest, most noxious and dangerous', was held in the Bull Ring. Its market concentrated on cattle, while sheep were sold in Corve Street and pigs at the top of Old Street.

The Bull Ring was also the scene of the 'barbarous and unmanly' practice of bull-baiting. A ferocious bull (or bear) was tethered by a stout steel chain to a strong post in a ring or inn-yard. Our 'rude forefathers' then gathered round to watch and bet as bull-dogs, one at a time, were set to bait the bull. The skill of the dogs, which in those days were long in the jaw and leg, was measured by their ability to pin the bull by the nose. It was quite a profitable business for the bull's keeper. He received two or three pence for three runs from each dog-owner and took a collection from the spectators. He usually had about him a piece of wood to lever open a dog's jaws which fastened too tightly on the bull. The animal could be baited three or four times a day, a collection being made each time. The landlord of one of the inns in the Bull Ring would hire the keeper and the bull or bear for three days for about ten shillings, in the hopeful expectation of increased trade. People of all classes watched the 'amusement', even on occasion members of the Corporation, dressed in their robes. Bull-baiting was a popular sport at wakes, while bear-baiting was sometimes held in celebration of a marriage.

In Ludlow bull-baiting was practised until the latter end of the 18th century although it was not stopped nationally until 1835. As the writer of a Ludlow guide said in 1822 'it is much to the credit of the inhabitants that this relic of barbarism, adopted by our ancestors, and

1—Ye Olde Bull Ring *   6—Elephant & Castle
2—Bear   7—Bull & Castle
3—Keysell's   8—Griffin
4—Salutation   9—Feathers *
5—Bull *   10—King's Arms

*—Open in 2002

The Bull Ring.

calculated to corrupt the heart and harden it against every tender feeling of humanity, is now discontinued here'.

Ye Olde Bull Ring Tavern at Nos. 43/44 Bull Ring comprises what used to be two separate timber-framed buildings on one of Ludlow's most ancient sites. In the 15th century the buildings were owned by Richard Malmshull, a merchant, when there was a wine cellar below. Over the years the premises were used by butchers, milliners, and a taxidermist, and in the 1880s became a wine and spirit merchants owned by Dawes & Bowen when its sign read 'Importers and dealers in foreign wines and spirits'. No. 43 was used as an ale store.

By 1901 it had become **The Vaults**, with an attached off-licence owned by the brewers Allsopp and Sons, of Burton-on-Trent, and run first by William Tanner, who later went to the **Feathers**, and later by a Mr. H.R. Hall. Three bars are listed together with a smoke room, market room and seven bedrooms. Stabling was available for two horses but was 'in bad repair, and requires whitewashing'. An advertisement showed Mr. Tanner, a keen horseman, selling proprietary whisky together with one called 'Ludlow Hunt'.

The front of No. 43 had been hidden behind Georgian stucco for many years, but in the 1930s it was stripped off and the two buildings became **Ye Olde Bull Ring Tavern**. In 1941 the landlord was Samuel A. Leach.

Next door at No. 45 was the **Bear** Inn (another reference to the sport of animal baiting), with an equally fine timber-framed frontage. It had become the **Bear** by the early 1630s, when the landlord, Thomas Hitchcox, was one of a small but influential circle of Ludlow Puritans formed mainly from local tradesmen. When he died in 1644 he bequeathed his soul to Almighty God trusting 'to be one of His elect' and an inheritor of 'the Kingdom of Heaven'. Thomas Hitchcott was

Ye Olde Bull Ring Tavern.
*The next two buildings adjoining it were the **Bear** and **Keysell's**.*

the almost identically named landlord towards the end of the 17th century. His time provides a fine example of how leading innkeepers often had high inventory values, for his goods were valued at £550 when he died in 1695. However, after his debts and other reductions had been made, this figure was reduced to £160.

Early in the 18th century David Valentine, landlord of the **Bear**, which possibly then had the constellation as its sign, was featured in the first issue of Ludlow's first known newspaper, *The Ludlow Postman*, on the occasion of his marriage to Mrs. Downes of the **Plough Inn** in Raven Lane. Valentine, a keen musician, was later to become organist at the Parish Church. He died in 1776. The report read:

> Ludlow, October 8th - Tuesday last being Valentine's Day (or the day Mr Valentine, Musician, put his hand to the Plough, in order for Seedness...) was celebrated a marriage between the said Mr Valentine and one Mrs Downs of the **Plough Inn** in this town; and with more Uncommon Splendour than hath been known by any of this Place, for going to church Mrs Bride was led up guarded by two Officers, and

85

Mr Bridegroom came next, attended by two ladies of the best Quality about this place, and after there followed a numerous Train of Gentlemen and Ladies in Couples, a Dragoon and his Spouse concluding the rear.

After the Nuptial Ceremonies were performed, the Company was entertained with a very handsome Dinner, and the whole Day was attended with Ringing of Bells, Musick and Dancing which they prolonged (to the general uneasiness of Mr Bridegroom) till 3 o'clock the next Morning; at which Time they concluded the Solemnity with Sock-Possets and the usual Custom of Throwing the stocking; and I hear many Persons have stood less pelted in the Pillory than they were on the Bed.

In 1790 the innkeeper was Robert Plowman. By 1814 the **Bear** had became a pharmacy and continued in this capacity for the next 150 years. By the turn of the century it was Woodhouse's chemist shop. Woodhouse was Mayor when the Princess of Wales, later Queen Mary, came to Ludlow in 1909, and her patronage of his shop—she apparently bought a tooth brush—entitled him to display the royal arms. It became Boots the Chemist in 1965. This four-storey building now has Jumper, a ladies clothes shop, on the ground floor with accommodation above.

The Wine Vaults at No. 46 held a licence from about 1800 but before that, in 1792, it was known as the **New Wine Cellars.** The first

---

46, BULL RING LUDLOW.

C. F. KEYSELL,

[LATE SHEPPARD & KEYSELL]

IMPORTER OF WINES AND SPIRITS

Agent for Allsopp's and Bass's Burton Ales, and Guinness's and Watkin's Dublin Stout.
Pale Ale and Dublin Stout in Cask or Bottle.

	Per Kilderkin.		Per Firkin
Pale (India) Ale .. .. . . 33s.		East India Pale Ale	16s 6d
Strong Ditto .. .. 30s.		Strong Ditto	15s 0d
Fine Mild Ale .. .. 27s.		Mild Ale	13s 6d
Mild Ale 24s		Ditto	12s 0d
Ditto .. .. 21s.		Ditto	10s 6d
Ditto .. .. 18s.		Ditto	9s 0d

Table Beer, 15s. per Kilderkin. Sound Beer at 8d. per gallon.
☞ The trade supplied direct from Burton, upon the same terms as those of the brewers in 36 18 and 9 gallon casks.
Detailed price list gratis upon application of Old-Landed Brandies, Whiskies, Old Ports, Sherries, Clarets, and Champagnes.

*1891 price list for **Keysell's**.*
A kilderkin is about 18 gallons; a firkin 9 gallons.

owner was Francis Massey and in 1901 it was still owned by an Elizabeth Massey, who lived in Winchester. It consisted of a bar, market room, and office. The business was run by Charles Francis Keysell, late of Sheppard and Keysell, a wine and spirit merchant established in 1780, which probably operated in Old Street. **Keysell's**, as it became known, became 'agent for Allsopp's and Bass's Burton ales, Guinness's celebrated Dublin stouts, pale ale and Dublin stout in bottle'. By 1926 it was advertised as 'wholesale and retail wine and spirit merchants, cigar importers, wine shippers, bonders and blenders, wholesale beer dealers, bottlers of beers and stout etc'. In 1958 it was

*Once the **Wine Vaults**, then **Keysell's**.*

described as a place 'where they still break down the spirits'. **Keysell's** became a favourite place for female imbibers as they could enter at the rear from a doorway in Pepper Lane without being seen. Now it houses a travel agent.

The **Salutation** (from the Latin *salutare*—to keep safe, to greet— and referring to the proclamation of Archangel Gabriel to the Virgin Mary, a sign much disliked by the Puritans) is believed to have been at No. 7, now Richards & Sons Ltd., ironmongers. In the 1680s it was run by John Morris Junior, son of John Morris, landlord at the newly opened **Feathers**. Morris, described as a vintner, stocked 'Canary,

Claret, white wine and Mallego' but also stocked beer, ale and cider. On his death in 1689 he left a probate inventory valued at £404 1s. 1d., but after deductions for debts and property leases it came to £194 16s. 9d. The **Salutation** must have closed early in the next century as there is no reference to it in the records of 1742 when the Licensing Act of George II was operational.

THE BULL HOTEL

The Bull has been an inn since the fifteenth century, when the formerly galleried range in the yard was erected. Remains of an earlier roof dating from c.1350 still exist in the main block of the building.

In the fifteenth century the premises were owned by some of the leading families of the town, and the Bull is first referred to by name in a will of 1580. In 1693 the inn was badly damaged when rioters attacked a Presbyterian meeting which was being held in the building. The frontage was completely destroyed by a fire in 1794, and subsequently rebuilt in the Georgian style.

A reminder that bull baiting took place in the Bull Ring is the **Bull Hotel**, at No. 14. The site probably dates back to the 12th century when St. Laurence's church was being built, thus making it one of Ludlow's oldest buildings. It may well have been built to refresh the workers constructing the church. The earliest known reference, however, is in 1319, when it was described as a tenement owned by Matthew Hopton. In 1343 it was known as Peter the Proctor's House, which extended from the street to the cemetery of St. Laurence.

It became an inn in the mid-15th century when the jettied timber-frame range, formerly galleried, was built, with the main block including the remains of a roof dating from about 1350. In 1482 the owners were the heirs of Roger Morton as was also the case in 1491 when the occupier was Thomas Cooke. In the 16th century the building was extended towards the church, with a number of the apartments including a stable for the horse and a room overhead for its owner, rather like a medieval motel. For the more genteel guests a fire, for warmth and cooking, could be obtained at extra cost. The **Bull** is first referred to by that name in a will of 1580 left by Simon Clare, the owner. From 1658 to 1689 it was owned by Thomas and Humphrey Crundall, with Thomas described as a London merchant. By 1667 it was described as having 12 hearths with Meredith Ness as innkeeper, who, having no wife, children or dependents, seemingly lived there on his own. He stayed there for 22 years.

It was in 1693, during the 14-year tenancy of innkeeper John Bingley, that the inn was badly damaged when rioters attacked a Presbyterian meeting being held there.

Will probates show that in 1734 the **Bull's** landlord, John Cropper, left £279 10s., but after deductions this came to only £109 10s. Towards the end of that century, the innkeeper, Richard Morgan, owner and occupier from 1794 to 1799, bequeathed the **Bull** to his brother William, also described as an innkeeper, and his brother-in-law Thomas Davenport, a baker. To his wife he left the sum of £20 a year.

*The courtyard of the **Bull** in 2001.*

Sometime between 1768 and 1794, ornate oak panels with six richly carved coats of arms of leading members of the Council in the Marches were removed from the chapel of St. Mary Magdalene in Ludlow Castle, then lying in ruins, They were taken to the **Bull** where they were installed in the upstairs dining room and enjoyed by guests until the early years of the 20th century. Two of the heraldic devices belonged to the eminent Elizabethans, Henry Herbert, earl of

*The **Bull** in 2001.*

Pembroke (1534-1601), who was Lord President of the Council in the Marches from 1586, and Sir John Pickering (1544-96), Justice of Carmarthen. The panels mysteriously disappeared in the late 1920s, and are believed to have been sold and exported to the United States.

In 1794 while Richard Morgan was still innkeeper a fire broke out resulting in the front façade being rebuilt in the Georgian style. From 1839 to 1843 the publican was William Pea, who was married with no children and kept four servants. In 1856 the landlord was Thomas Crane who was succeeded by his widow Catherine Crane (1870-1909), by which time the **Bull** was described as 'a family and commercial hotel'.

In a return of licensed houses in Ludlow in 1901, the **Bull Hotel** was described as having a bar, parlour, smoke room, kitchen and seven bedrooms. It had stabling for nine horses. Catherine Crane was still the owner and occupier and the rateable value was £40 15s. It was then described as an 'agricultural and commercial hotel'.

An advertisement in 1926 boasted that the **Bull** had 'electric light throughout with special accommodation for excursionists and tourists'. It was also the headquarters of the Castle Bowling and Tennis Club and had a billiards room. Its telephone number was 12 and the proprietor was Arthur Wall. In 1968 it was bought by the brewers' Marston, Thompson and Evershed.

*A procession outside the **Bull** and the **Elephant and Castle** about 1900.*

90

It was about 1975, that internal alterations revealed a well and a flight of about 11 steps pointing towards the churchyard, together with a secret room above a fireplace that is presumed to be a priest's hole. This could be the explanation of some ghostly happenings; mysterious footsteps, which have been heard, are often attributed to a priest checking up on the occupants of 'his house'. Mr. Chris Barrack, the then newly-arrived owner/landlord, had 'felt' a ghost on two occasions. After a row with his wife, Mr. Barrack went downstairs to open for the evening. Still annoyed about the tiff he suddenly felt a hand on his shoulder. Thinking it was his wife he turned round, but there was no-one there. Three months later he felt a hand on his shoulder once more, but again no-one was in sight. The landlord, who said the grip was somehow reassuring, thought that the hand belonged to the ghost of an old woman who, according to nearby residents, manifested herself to any newcomers to the area of the **Bull**.

Phil and Sally Maile, who took over in 1988, have also experienced some strange happenings. Sally has seen an old man and a little girl at the foot of her bed in the night, heavy fire doors have burst open and banged against the wall, burglar alarms have gone off, and things have disappeared only to reappear. Shortly after Phil saw a man walk across the car park and disappear three years ago, ghost-hunters were brought in, but despite an over-night vigil nothing 'ghostly' was reported.

The **Bull** was bought in 1999 by the Wolverhampton and Dudley Brewery with the Mailes as leaseholders. Every year they hold a fringe festival, including four days of international jazz and a week of fringe events, which coincides with the Ludlow Festival. Among other

The 1924 bank building that replaced the ***Elephant and Castle***.

*The annual tug-of-war between the **Feathers** (left) and the **Bull** (right).*

events are live music, Morris Men, brass band competitions, and the traditional Boxing Day 'tug-of-war' competition across the main road versus the **Feathers Hotel**. The tug-of-war is won by the team achieving the best of three pulls.

Looking at the National Westminster Bank at No. 15, next door to **The Bull,** one would not have been at all suprised to learn that here once stood an equally fine inn—the **Elephant and Castle.** However, the inn itself was demolished in 1924 to make way for this completely new bank building. The earliest known reference to the site was in 1360 when John de Pusselowe 'raised a chamber outside the door of his Hall in Corve Street' (this part of the Bull Ring was known as Corve Street in the Middle Ages). Fourteen years later this same John de Pusselowe passed on the property to Richard de Masbrook, draper, together with a tenement in Corve Street within Corve Gate, stretching from the street to the graveyard.

The Palmers' Guild became the owners in 1482 and let it out to David Adams 'where he dwells' for 20s. In 1669 it was described as 'ye new building joining to the Bull', a timber-framed building having been erected in about 1662, and owned by Thomas Crundall, a London merchant, who also owned the **Bull**. It went on to become one of the top six hotels in Ludlow in the 18th century. At the beginning of the 19th century local guide books set out the principal inns of Ludlow with the **Elephant and Castle** in third place, behind the **Crown** and the **Angel**. The name, incidentally, was probably derived from the crest of the Cutler's Company which shows an elephant with a howdah on its back, the latter looking like a miniature castle.

The **Elephant and Castle** is mentioned in a publication called *Going to Markets and Grammar Schools, 1830-70* by George Griffiths, a corn merchant. It contains a description of a journey he made in 1837 from Bewdley to Ludlow. He dined at the **Elephant and Castle** where 'such a fine healthy set of tenants of the soil were seldom to be met with as that table' though 'they grumbled a bit at something or other—either prices were too low, although the harvest was abundant, or the yield was too short, although the price was high'. The landlord then was probably Arthur Evans. He was definitely there in 1841 with his wife, two children, three other adults and two servants. But two years later it was owned by the Borough Council with William Jennings the leaseholder at 20s. a year.

Various functions were held at the **Elephant and Castle** including a dinner at half past two on 26 May 1871, organised by the churchwardens of St. Laurence's following 'a perambulation of the boundary of the Parish'.

The return of licensed houses in 1901 described the **Elephant and Castle** as having a bar, commercial room, smokeroom, dining-room, parlour, kitchen, and six bedrooms. There was stabling for five horses. The landlady was Ellen Raiswell. The front at some point in its history was rendered with stucco and it was only when it was being stripped prior to demolition and half-timbering was revealed that the great age of the building was realised. But by then it was too late. Its spacious yard is now incorporated into that of the **Bull's**, doubling the size of that establishment's.

On the opposite side of the Bull Ring at Nos. 20 and 21, during the 17th and 18th centuries, was the **Bull and Castle**. Part of it now belongs to the **Feathers** and there are two ground-floor shops—The Feathers Gallery and Foxwoods Curios. In 1619 it had been the half burgage plot of Jermayn Season, but it later became licensed premises. On his death in 1726 the innkeeper, Richard Powford, left a probate inventory valued at £76 10s. In 1733 the innholder, Jeremiah Sayce, left an inventory worth £177 7s. 4d.

The adjoining premises, Nos. 22 and 23, was the site of the **Griffin Inn** (a fabulous monster, supposedly the offspring of a lion and an eagle, which kept guard over hidden treasures and became the badge of Edward III), a medium sized inn with seven hearths in the 16th and 17th centuries. The records of the local Court Leet show that in 1555 Alice Tranter, the proprietress, was presented for 'scolding upon John Season and his wife'. Season, a fletcher, was apparently the owner of the **Feathers** at that time. Later it was occupied by an innkeeper called Jarvis Dawson.

In 1620 it was was bought by Rees Jones, owner of the **Feathers** next door, and 50 years before that property became an inn. It was rebuilt in the 1670s. It was probably Thomas Jones II who decided about 1710 to close the **Griffin** and to use its rear premises as additional stabling for the **Feathers**. When it was closed the front part of the premises were occupied by a series of tradesmen. From 1758 until the mid-19th century the tenants were always blacksmiths. Between 1837 and 1846 the old **Griffin** was replaced by a three-storey

*A sketch of the **Feathers** in 1846.*

94

brick building, with a ground-floor shop and arched entrance to the yard behind. The front part of the **Griffin** was in separate ownership between 1870 and 1898, but is now owned by the **Feathers** who lease out a shop currently run as 'Climb on Bikes'.

The **Feathers Hotel**, at Nos. 20 to 24 Bull Ring, was described by Pevsner as 'that prodigy of timber-framed houses' and in an 1894 travel book as 'perhaps as fine an example of black and white timbered building as may be found anywhere', whilst Maisie Herring commented 'at first glance you feel that it cannot be real; the gorgeous corbelling and balustrading must have come off some studio set after all'.

The original building, which is no. 24, has been an inn since 1670 and before that was a private dwelling dating probably as far back as the 15th century, but certainly to 1544 when it was owned by Thomas Hakluyt, Clerk of the Council in the Marches and a relation of Richard, author of *The Principal Navigations, Voyages, Traffics and Discoveries of the English Nation.*

The Recorder of Ludlow, Edward Waties, and his wife Martha (to whom there is a monument in St. Laurence's Church), were the next owners. They sold it for £225 in 1619 to Rees Jones, from Pembrokeshire, who became one of Ludlow's wealthiest citizens and an attorney at the courts of the Council in the Marches. He commissioned the refronting and enlargement of the house, bringing in craftsmen to construct the richly decorated façade which is still one of Ludlow's main attractions.

Still surviving is the main door, with its 350 iron studs, although it was repositioned in the 1830s. On the lockplate are the initials 'R. I.' for Rees Jones and the smaller initials 'I. I.' for his wife Isabel. Also instantly recognisable are the three pairs of ostrich feathers on the collars of the three street gables, which were carved at the same time and from which the building derives its name. Feathers are traditionally the badge of the Prince of Wales and as such have been included in the Borough Arms of Ludlow, making the point that three heirs to the throne—Edward, son of Edward IV; Arthur, son of Henry VII; and Mary, daughter of Henry VIII—all resided at Ludlow Castle. Also, celebrations had been held in Ludlow in 1616 when Charles, James I's eldest son, was invested Prince of Wales at Whitehall.

During the Civil War Rees Jones moved out to his other house in Sheet and the **Feathers**, which had eight empty rooms and nine hearths, was billeted out to Royalist soldiers.

It was not until about 1670 that the **Feathers** became an inn, a decision taken by Thomas Jones I, Rees Jones' heir. Being on the main north to south road and close to the Beast Market, it was in an ideal position, witness all the other inns in the vicinity. The first landlord was John Morris, who died in 1687, leaving £296 15s., but which after deductions came to only £51 10s., still a sizeable amount in those days. Drunkenness was common as in 1714 when 'Hooper of The Feathers was presented at court for an affront upon the body of Francis Pearson'.

An advertisement for a new landlord appeared in the *Birmingham Gazette* in 1749, which described the **Feathers Inn** as 'being an accustomed house, and one of the best in the said town, having a large cover'd Cock-pit, and stabling for above one hundred horses, with other conveniences suitable to a large inn'. The site of the cock-pit, mentioned again when the property was sold in 1787, is not known, but cock-fighting was practised there for much of the 18th century.

The heiress of Robert Jones, his unmarried niece, sold the **Feathers** in 1787 to the landlord, John Rogers, for £480. Rogers had been landlord since 1773. In 1805 it was sold to John Griffiths, a butcher.

Prize-fighting was another violent sport presented at the **Feathers** in the 1820s when James Hosie was landlord. It was

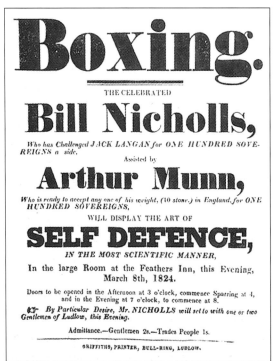

*Boxing at the **Feathers** in 1824.*

held in the large room previously used for billiards and proved very popular. There were quite a few 'rare treats for the fancy'.

Nicholls was the son of Nonpareil George and had 'defeated Crib at Blackwater'. Other pugilists who displayed their skills at the **Feathers** included Ingliss, 'the feather bed maker who fought Ned Turner and is about to fight again with Turner'. This same James Hosie 'declined business' in September 1824 when he tendered 'his grateful thanks to the inhabitants of Ludlow, and the public, generally, for the very liberal support received by him'.

His successor, Robert Pickering: 'humbly solicits the patronage of the Friends of his predecessor, and the public, especially those gentlemen who have so long supported the House, assuring them of his unremitting attention to their comforts; he has laid in a choice stock of wines and spirits, and feels confident in his ability to serve his friends well'. Pickering concluded: 'The excellent stabling of this inn will be carefully attended to, by one experienced, civil and steady ostler'.

Like other inns, the **Feathers** served the needs of the community. Various functions were held there including public auctions and on market days farmers could use a Market Room on the ground floor. The inn also supported horse-racing at the Bromfield track.

In the mid-19th century the inn was also active as an electioneering centre. Ludlow used to be a 'pocket borough' when the M.P.s were either a Herbert of Oakly Park, or a Clive (descendants of Robert) chosen by a few burgesses. After the Reform Act of 1832 the franchise was given to 350 householders each worth £10 or more and political activity became frantic with bribery common. The most notorious election was that of 1839, caused by the succession of Lord Clive to the earldom of Powis. 'Vital transactions' took place at the **Feathers** and one voter received £300 in bribes. The first-floor balcony was built for electioneering purposes a few years afterwards, as from here the parliamentary candidate, who used the **Feathers** as his temporary abode, would address the electors.

The inn was sold in 1836 to Henry Whittall, druggist and later banker, who became mayor of Ludlow in 1844. Between 1849 and 1861, a horse-drawn omnibus, known as the Red Rover, left the inn three times a week to go to Knighton, on the Welsh border. The inn was put up for sale again in 1870, when it was bought by Robert Edwards, formerly

THE FEATHERS,

FIRST CLASS FAMILY & COMMERCIAL HOTEL AND POSTING HOUSE.

CHARLES EDWARDS · · PROPRIETOR.

ONE OF THE OLDEST ESTABLISHED COMMERCIAL HOUSES IN THE KINGDOM.

BILLIARD AND SMOKING ROOMS.

Wedding and Funeral Carriages, Hearses, New Funeral Car with Glass or Panelled Sides, Flys, Broughams, Brakes, Private Omnibuses, Post and Saddle Horses let on the shortest notice and on reasonable terms.

GOOD ACCOMMODATION FOR HUNTERS AND GENTLEMEN'S HORSES.

OMNIBUS MEETS ALL TRAINS.

LUDLOW, SHROPSHIRE.

*1891 advertisement for the **Feathers**.*

landlord of the **Angel**, who was three times mayor of Ludlow. Edwards, and later his son Charles, helped to establish the **Feathers** as one of the leading hotels in the area.

In 1898 the lease passed to the Church Stretton Hotel Company, controlled by Southams of Shrewsbury, 'ale, porter and spirit merchants', and an extensive restoration of the interior was carried out. In 1901, when it was run by Harriet Beard, it comprised a bar, bar parlour, two smoke rooms, Market Room, commercial room, coffee room, billiard room, sitting, drawing and dining rooms, and 21 bedrooms. There was stabling, described as being in good repair and clean, for 16 horses. The

*The sitting room at the **Feathers** around 1900.*

rateable value was £282, nearly twice the amount of the **Angel**.

*1926 advertisement for the **Feathers**.*

The Feathers Hotel, LUDLOW

Telegrams "TANNER, LUDLOW"
TELEPHONE P.O. 19

High-Class Family and
- Commercial Hotel -
and Posting House.

Large Yard, Excellent Loose Boxes and Stables.

Within easy reach of
Four Packs of Hounds.

Good Hunting Quarters.   Omnibus meets all trains.   Garage,
Inspection Pits, Petrol, etc.   Hunters for Hire.

W. TANNER, Proprietor.

After the Church Stretton company went bankrupt, the **Feathers** was bought at public auction in 1909 by William Tanner, former landlord of the **Bull Ring Tavern**. Tanner was also a tenant farmer and secretary of the local hunt and, perhaps not surprisingly, advertisements refer to 'good hunting quarters' and describe the hotel as 'within easy reach of four packs of hounds'. In 1910 it received the accolade of a royal visit with Prince Henry of Prussia, brother of the German emperor and first cousin of King Edward VII, 'partaking of tea'.

The impact of the car was the outstanding feature of the Tanner years. Two garages had already opened in Ludlow by 1910, but it was a gradual transition.

*The dining room at the **Feathers** about 1910.*

Until 1939 the Feathers' omnibus was still horse-drawn and the hotel claimed that every train was met. Sometimes its pair of horses was put to other uses, being hired out for weddings and funerals and even for the town's fire-engine. In 1947 it had stabling for 13 horses as well as garaging for eight cars.

Tanner called a meeting of the Ludlow and District Licensed Victuallers' Association at the **Feathers** on 29 December 1931 to resuscitate the old Association which for some time past had practically ceased to exist. Tanner was elected President and 26 members joined at an annual subscription of 10s. The question of the stopping of games in licensed premises by the police was raised.

In *Footsteps Down Mill Street*, George Merchant, president of the Old Ludloverians Club, gives a first hand account of the Tanners. 'Bill Tanner, a great connoisseur of his own wares and somewhat crusty in consequence, held court in the long bar, seated in his special chair by the grandfather clock. He rose only to replenish his glass and, less frequently, to abuse and pursue to the door customers of whom he did not approve, especially coach parties and unaccompanied women. His wife, a much milder character, presided inside the magnificent dining room upstairs over a succulent cold table, of which she was rightly proud'.

It was Kathleen, Tanner's widow, who ran the hotel during the Second World War when

*The **Feathers** in the 1930s.*

100

*Overmantle at the **Feathers**.*

food and male staff were in short supply, but the presence of nearby British and American military camps helped to keep up demand for the hotel's services.

After 35 years being run by the Tanners, the **Feathers** was sold in 1947 for £30,000 to a specially constituted company headed by Ralph Edwards, a businessman from Droitwich. He never lived in Ludlow and the day-to-day running of the **Feathers** was entrusted to managers. Among these were Bill and Kitty Shelley, who had 'a bevy of handsome, dark-eyed daughters'. When the Americans moved on, newcomers appeared including Mac Westmeads. He was:

> a dashing character, tall and moustachioed with a mighty thirst acquired on service in India. He was a great man for the horses and had the unusual habit of celebrating not when he won but when he lost, a not infrequent occurrence. He would then drown his sorrows, with many willing helpers, and for their entertainment would demonstrate that when under the influence he was impervious to pain. He would crush tumblers between his teeth, which were admittedly false, and put on the blazing bar fire his bare feet, which were real, and sizzled. He would then take his watch and chain and try to swallow them, friends hauling on the chain when he became blue in the face.

In 1986 the hotel became a private company run by Osmond Edwards, Ralph's younger brother, his wife Margaret and their four children.

The restoration of the façade was started in 1969 and won a Civic Trust award in 1971. Nos. 20 and 21 were acquired in 1970 to allow expansion and in 1983 No. 25 was purchased. Behind the latter's late 18th-early 19th-century street front, this property has been completely rebuilt to accommodate the Comus bar, a medium-sized conference room and three bedroom suites.

From the size and position of the King James I lounge, it is clear that it was originally the great chamber used by Rees Jones. The room has low ceilings with ornate plasterwork designs and the plain oak wall panelling concentrates attention on the fireplace and its overmantel, probably not installed until 1846. It bears the coat of arms of King James I—hence the room's name. On the same floor is the Edward IV writing room, also with oak-panelling and carved mantel. Besides 40 en-suite bedrooms the hotel has a large restaurant, and the Prince Charles and Prince William banqueting suites.

*The **Feathers** empire now includes 21, 23 and 25 Bull Ring.*

Corus and Regal Hotels bought the **Feathers** from the late Osmond Edwards some five years ago and late in 2001 the hotel was once again on the market, this time with an asking price of £1,750,000. It has since been purchased by West Bromwich businessman, Sam Ceney.

Records show that the **King's Arms** at No. 35 dates back to the 17th century, but it was probably older as it stood on an ancient site leading down towards the old Galdeford Gate. It is mentioned during the Civil War (1642-51) when local public opinion was hostile to those

*The **King's Arms** is now a shop.*

*The **King's Arms**.*

who flaunted Parliamentary beliefs. Indeed, Thomas Vaughan, of Tewkesbury, who was 'well affected to Parliament', was unable to collect his rent from the **King's Arms** in the Bull Ring without 'great danger or hazard to life'.

In the next century the **King's Arms** was divided into two messuages one still called the **King's Arms** and the other the **Boot and Shoe**, with several other messuages built on part of the yard or converted from the brewhouse and laundry. In 1790 the innkeeper was John Ballard. In the 19th century one of the licensees was Edward Collier, also a gardener, who had 11 children. The youngest child was Mary Jones who, in 1903 when she was aged 93, decided to publish the 'Reminiscences of an old inhabitant (1809-1830)' in the *Ludlow Advertiser*. In 1859 the inn was run by Ann Owen.

In 1888 Thomas Swarbrick was the landlord and also the 'refreshment room keeper'. He was probably still in charge in 1890 when a case was brought for selling drink to a drunken person, but it was dismissed. In 1901 it was called **Ye Old King's Arms** when the owner and occupier had the delightful name John Bytheway. The narrow, three-storey building comprised a bar, kitchen, parlour, dining room and four bedrooms. There was stabling for one horse.

By 1910 it had reverted to **King's Arms** with the addition of 'Dining Rooms'. It also offered 'home brew'd ales'. It closed soon after trade began to get back to normal after the First World War. It then became a butcher's shop with a greengrocery added and a café at the rear. Today it is an Edinburgh Woollen Mill shop.

CHAPTER EIGHT

Market Street & Raven Lane

Although only a short stretch of road, Market Street at one time boasted no fewer than five licensed houses—it now has only one. Before 1870 the name of the street was Hand and Bell Lane, the same name as one of the pubs; even earlier it was known as Barnes Row, apparently derived from Barons Row.

On the corner of Broad Street and Market Street once stood the **Tavern**, where ale used to be dispensed from the cellar. It must have been one of Ludlow's earliest pubs, but there is no mention of it after the 16th century. A branch of Lloyds TSB now stands on the site.

Further along Market Street at No. 7, where the bakers R. Walton Ltd. now trade, was once the **Grape Vaults**, which, from its name, probably originally sold wine and spirits from its cellar. From at least 1792 it held a full six-day license. In a directory of 1859 it was described as just the **Grapes** with John Sawyer as licensee, and is mentioned in another directory of 1868. Towards the end of the century the inn was getting into some trouble with the law. In October 1895 the landlord was fined 40s. with costs of 20s. 6d. for 'selling drink to a drunken person'. Then in April 1899 a case was brought for selling adulterated brandy, but this was dismissed.

In the 1901 return of licensed houses for Ludlow, the **Grape Vaults** was described as a free house owned by Henry Gatehouse of Dinham and occupied by George Millward—the third landlord in five years. The pub, with a rateable value of £23 7s. 6d., consisted of a bar, parlour, smoke room, kitchen and three bedrooms. There was no stabling.

A few years later the **Grape Vaults** lost its license, apparently during a purge to reduce the number of licensed premises in Ludlow.

1—Tavern   6—Raven
2—Grape Vaults   7—Borough Arms
3—Hand & Bell   8—Plough
4—Globe*   9—Wagon & Horses
5—Old Red Lion   10—Prince of Wales
        *—*Open in 2002*

The following were also in Raven Lane,
but their positions are unknown:
        Plume of Feathers
        Turk's/Saracen's Head
        Goat's Head

Market Street & Raven Lane.

The local magistrates were said to have been particularly hard on pubs where the landlord had previous convictions.

If the **Grape Vaults** was relatively small, the **Hand & Bell** was even smaller, consisting of just the one bar. The name probably originated from hand bell ringing. It is mentioned in the *Universal British Directory* of 1790 when the licensee was Thomas Hill, and in another directory of 1822. The licensee in 1859 was James White and in 1888 it was William Raiswell. The licensing returns of 1901 show that the **Hand & Bell** was a tied house owned by Ind Coope and Co. with the occupier given as Donald Anderson. The property had a rateable value of £15 5s. and comprised a bar, kitchen, parlour, sitting-room and six bedrooms. There was no stabling. The license was renewed in 1911, but soon after the First World War the inn had closed down. Today the **Hand & Bell** premises are occupied by a dental surgery.

No. 7 Market Street,
*once the **Grapes Tavern**.*

Next door to the **Hand & Bell**, and the sole surviving pub in Market Street, is the **Globe Inn**, which is linked to a number of ghost stories. One of the earliest tales refers to a murder which apparently took place at the inn in the 16th century. A Tudor soldier called Edward Dobson, who was stationed at Ludlow Castle, is reputed to have died during a pub brawl in 1553. His ghost, a bewigged figure with a cloak around his shoulders, is said 'to hover around the spot of his demise'. It could have been the ghost of Dobson, said to have died in an upstairs room, who scared four young people staying at the hotel in 1954. They reported seeing a 'spectral visitor with a cloak around his body and a wig on his head'. Another version describes the ghost as being clad in a leather jerkin with some sort of helmet on his head.

*Once the **Hand and Bell**, but now a dental surgery. The flags are from the **Globe** celebrating the World Cup.*

Then there is the story of the 'Gentleman' ghost. It was seen by Roma Jones in 1914 when, as a school girl, she stayed with her aunt Georgina and uncle George Lunn who were running the inn. Writing in the *Shropshire Magazine* of 1956, she described how she awoke one stormy night and on going for some water she saw an elderly man holding a candlestick. When she asked: 'Who are you?' a quavering voice replied: 'It's only me'. It was only later that she discovered she had seen 'the famous

An 1891 advertisement for the **Globe**.

Globe Ghost'. She wrote: 'I shall never forget that pale face, with its white, longish hair and the tassel on his nightcap falling to his shoulder, resting on his night shirt, and his hand holding the brass candlestick with its lighted candle'. The ghost has also been described as an amiable old gentleman in a Georgian coat who seems 'to be quite non-scaring to children'.

The inn was originally known as the **Red Lion**, but the house next door, on the corner with Raven Lane, was also called the **Red Lion** although the latter did add **Old** to its name. Thus, in a directory of 1822, there are two **Red Lions** listed for Barnes Row. There was probably strong competition between the two inns and in the 1850s the **Red Lion** changed its name to the **Globe**.

The **Globe's** old cobblestone yard was once known as the Steelyard, where, in an out-building by the stables, an iron foundry produced nails. The yard was also where Ludlow's official weights and measures were kept. It was here that standard weights, yard measures and bushels were once tested, and any brewer, baker or butcher who either gave short measure or adulterated food or drink had to suffer the indignity of the gumble or ducking stool. Originally the culprit was hoisted up at the end of a long beam and pelted with rotten fruit, refuse and bad eggs; it was only later that it was transformed into a ducking stool, which was also used to 'punish' women who were scolds or who nagged.

A **Red Lion** was mentioned in a list of licensed houses of 1750 and again in 1792. William Coats was given as the landlord in 1859. In

Porter's Directory of the County of Salop of 1888, a list of publicans with their trades shows that the licensee James Oakes was not only a brewer but also a painter and plumber.

The **Globe** was also a centre for carriers' carts. In 1894, for instance, there were nine departures a week carrying people and goods to and from neighbouring villages such as Ashford, Hope and Wilde, for the Ludlow markets.

A licensing review of 1901 shows that the **Globe** had a full licence, granted in 1840, and that it comprised a bar, parlour, smoke room, taproom, and six bedrooms. There was stabling for 10 horses. The inn, which had a rateable value of £34, was owned by Ann Oakes of Market Street, and the landlady was Sarah Davies. The nature of its trade was

*The **Globe**, half hidden down the narrow Market Street.*

described as agricultural and in town. Ludlow Football Club, whose secretary was John Parsonage, used the inn as its headquarters.

By the start of the First World War the **Globe** was run by the Lunns and still had its own brewhouse, serving its own home-brewed ale. Roma Jones recalled: 'I remember our bedroom was built over the brewhouse where every second Monday Jim Devy came at 4 a.m. and lighted the fire under the huge copper where, when the water boiled, malt, hops and barley were added and a sweet boiling beer smell permeated through the house'. She also remembered that on cold nights beer was mulled with a red-hot poker, paper spills stood in cracked pint mugs on the mantelpiece and plates of bread and cheese were offered free of charge.

In 1926, Walter Charles Nash was the landlord, and in 1934 it was George Sydney Hiles, who died in 1954 at the age of 70 after 20 years at the pub. When the present landlord and landlady arrived some 12 years ago, ghostly happenings continued—their daughter found her bedroom door locked by itself, and guests staying on the top floor found doors regularly opening at 8 o'clock at night.

On the other side of the **Globe**, on the corner of Raven Lane, was the rival **Red Lion**, which had changed its name to **Old Red Lion** by 1840. From 1763 a coach ran regularly between Ludlow and London via Worcester, and by 1779 it left the **Red Lion** at 6 a.m. on Tuesday, reaching London 'early the next day'. It was described as one of Ludlow's principal inns in a town guide of 1822.

To confuse matters further the inn was originally called the **New Crown**, because of its proximity to the **Crown** in Broad Street. Its yard had sets of buildings, each consisting of one room down and one up,

*The **Old Red Lion** or **New Crown** was on the corner with Raven Lane.*

used by the grooms of the well-to-do clients who stayed at the **Crown**, with whose yard its own connected at right angles.

In the early part of the 19th century the **New Crown**, by then called the **Red Lion Inn**, was sold by William Walker to Richard Wakefield. Walker, obviously an entrepreneur, had already sold off part of the inn's property. Records for 1813 show that one part, which was described as a malthouse, maltkiln, cistern, privy and cellars under the malthouse and which he had converted into two dwellings and 'a malthouse by adding several new erections' had been sold. The purchaser of the malthouse part was to have the use of the yard and an access through the back-way into Raven Lane, in common with Wakefield's tenant, and also the use of a pump.

The purchaser, Mr. Edward Rea, who was also innkeeper of the **Talbot** in Tower Street, soon put it on the market, for in March 1823 an auction was held at the **George Inn** for the sale of:

> [the] compact freehold messuage, or dwelling house with a spacious malthouse adjoining ... The whole of the premises are in complete repair, having been newly erected within these few years; the Malthouse has commodious bins for storing malt, and is abundantly supplied with water from a pump within it, and sufficiently large to admit of 3,000 bushels being made therein in the course of a season.

No sale seemed to have been made, however, and two years later another auction was held—this time at the **Talbot Inn**—when the house and malthouse were offered as one of three lots. The house was tenanted and the malthouse was 'in work'.

Four months later, in June 1825, the malthouse and dwelling were once again put up for sale by auction at the **Talbot Inn**. A poster, headed 'to Malsters and others', proclaimed that a:

> desirable freehold messuage, malthouse & premises, in excellent repair, to be (peremptorily) sold by Auction by Mr Bach, under a release for the benefit of creditors ... All that neat, convenient, substantial and well built dwelling house, together with a spacious substantial and newly erected Malthouse thereto adjoining, with the appurtenances, situated close to the **Old Red Lion Inn**, on the east side and nearly at the top of the Raven Lane, late in the possession of Mr. Edward Rea, maltster, but now in the occupation of Mr. Jeremiah Bach and Mr. Thomas George, as yearly tenants.

The Messuage has been recently erected and consists of a kitchen, parlour, brewhouse, pantry etc. on the ground floor and four good lodging rooms over, with excellent cellarage underneath the kitchen, and is well supplied with water.

The Malthouse is capable of wetting and drying upwards of 60 bushels, has an abundant supply of water, with every other requisite, and has been in constant work for many years past. The whole of the Premises are freehold, and being situated contiguous to the Corn Market, form a most desirable situation to any person wishing to engage in the malting business.

The malthouse was apparently unsuccessful, and by 1856 it had been turned into a carpenter's shop. In 1859 the landlord of the **Red Lion** was Timothy Price, who stayed there until 1877 when the inn stopped trading. Before that time came, however, he had to send for the police when one of his customers had drunk too much. The *Ludlow Advertiser*, in 1862, reported that P.C. Merryman was sent to the inn and asked to remove a Henry Brown who was creating a disturbance. Brown became very violent and took hold of Merryman by the hair and tore a piece from his coat. With the assistance of P.C. Dee he was taken to the Tower (the prison in Tower Street), but on the way kicked Dee severely. Later, in court, Brown was ordered to pay a 7s. 6d. fine, 12s. 6d. costs and 5s. damage or in default would face 14 days imprisonment with hard labour.

By 1877 there was no **Old Red Lion** and Timothy Price had become licensee of the **Plough** in adjacent Raven Lane. Traces remained, for until the 1970s one door of the building, long since converted into two shops with flats above, had a cast iron sign of a lion with the words **Old Red Lion** beneath. The corner shop premises is now Reg Martin & Sons, the popular butcher's, while the other one, adjacent to the **Globe**, sells ladies' lingerie.

Today there is little reason for the visitor to seek out Raven Lane, or Narrow Lane as it used to be called, with its tucked away entrance between Market and Castle Streets leading to terraced houses on either side. But a century or more ago it would have been a lively place, particularly on market days, with customers looking for refreshment at the numerous licensed houses.

The first port of call would have been the **Raven**, named after the bird which was sacred to the Druids, but later came to represent an unpleasant omen. The raven was also used in some coats of arms and it is said that in the late 17th century, after the revolution of 1688, it indicated Jacobite sympathies on the part of the innkeeper.

Judging by the existing premises at Nos. 16 to 19, now divided into two residences, the **Raven** must have been a substantial inn with stabling, although the latter would have been limited. It is first mentioned in a list of inns for 1742 and in a directory of 1790 the landlord was named as William Jackson and in 1859 it was Benjamin Milner. He may have been the last landlord, for

*The **Raven** is now two houses, but at one time it must have been a substantial hostelry.*

by the early 1860s the inn had ceased trading. Interestingly, another **Raven**, at the Sand Pits, had already opened for business by at least 1859 and continues to trade.

Last of the Raven Lane pubs to close, soon after the end of the Second World War, was the **Borough Arms** further down at No. 23. The name generally refers to a pub which stands on the borough boundary or was a stop for parties engaged in the ancient 'beating the bounds' ceremony, but in this case it appears to be neither. This inn could originally have been called the **Plumbers Arms**.

Licensing returns for 1901 showed that the **Borough Arms** had a full license dating back to about 1841. The owner was John Williams, of

Kempton, and the occupier Jonathan Cadwallader, who had been there for at least five years. Described as a market house, it comprised a bar parlour, kitchen and three bedrooms. There was no stabling. A directory of 1868 shows that the landlord was John Reynolds and in 1888 it was John Merryman.

By 1926 the licensee was Mrs. Lucy Mary Beeston with Arthur Evans taking over soon after. Harry Baker described, in his book on Ludlow pubs, how, as a trainee reporter on the *Ludlow Advertiser* in the 1930s, he knew Arthur Evans, who also worked as that paper's linotype operator. He was 'a fierce

*The **Plough** and the **Borough Arms** were adjacent pubs in Raven Lane.*

little man' and the **Borough Arms** was 'a fearsome place' to visit!

> At the end of the day he [Arthur] would put on his jacket and depart with the most dreadful imprecations and threats about what he would do to anyone disturbing him at home. There often came crisis times when the Editor must have Arthur Evans back ... and he would despatch me to the **Borough Arms** with the most dire threats of what would happen to me if I didn't bring him. At the sight of my entrance, Mr. Evans would almost dance with rage and tell me to go back and tell the Editor various unmentionable things ... I used to stand between the Butter Cross and the Bull Ring wondering, on the day's form, which one to offend.

After Evans' death during the war, his widow continued at the **Borough Arms** for a time, but the inn closed when she left. She died in the late 1970s at the age of 100. It is now a private house.

Next door to the **Borough Arms** at No. 24 was the **Plough**, which was equally small with just the one bar. The name is one of the most frequently met among pubs showing the sign of either the farm implement or the group of seven stars in the *Ursa Major* constellation which looks like a plough.

The first mention of the inn seems to be in the early 18th century when a report in the *Ludlow Postman* (a kind of early *Private Eye*) records that David Valentine, landlord of the **Bear** in the Bull Ring, 'put his hand to the Plough' in getting married to Mrs. Downes, of the **Plough Inn**. Samuel George is given as the licensee in a directory of 1790. The pub is mentioned in 1823 and in 1859 the licensee was Charles Yapp. By 1888 the landlord was another Charles, this time Pitt.

In 1901, the **Plough** was owned by Thomas Sheldon, of the Bull Ring, and the licensee was John Wright. Consisting of a bar, kitchen and six bedrooms with a rateable value of £16, it had a full license dating back to about 1840. Trade was described as agricultural and in town. A case for selling adulterated whisky in 1892 had been brought against a previous landlord, the licensing report stated, but it had been dismissed.

Ten years later the landlord Charles Biddell had to apply for the renewal of the **Plough**'s licence, as was reported in the *Ludlow Advertiser* of 4 March 1911. Superintendent Perry, the town's head of police, who objected, said the inn had been licensed since 1840. It consisted of a bar, kitchen and six bedrooms and had no stabling. There was no urinal, but it had a W.C. at the back, which appeared to be used by the family and the customers. He stated that the licence had been transferred three times within the last five years, and felt that little trade was done at the house, indeed, he had been in Ludlow for 20 years and he did not think there had been much trade done in all this time. He also noted that the licensee was working on a farm, at least he had been the day before the hearing. Within 600 yards there were 26 full licences and within a radius of 140 yards there were nine fully licensed houses without the **Plough**. The nearest house was the **Borough Arms** which adjoined the **Plough** and he stated that all these houses had equal if not better accommodation.

Expanding his area of consideration, he said that there were 39 pubs and one beer house in the borough, serving a population in 1901 of 6,328. That gave one hostelry to about every 158 persons. He agreed, however, that the population had considerably increased in 1901 as the Birmingham waterworks were in full swing and there was a large number of people in the town employed on that work. The **Plough** had accommodation for brewing their own beer but Supt. Perry did not know whether they did. Defence for Biddell said it was a free house and they brewed their own beer, which he believed was a desirable thing. In the event, a provisional licence was granted.

Although given a reprieve, the **Plough**'s number was virtually up and at the beginning of the 1920s the inn closed its doors for good leaving the landlord free to continue his farm work.

Towards the end of Raven Lane, still on the west side, are the towering, half-timbered premises which once housed an inn called the **Wagon & Horses**. It is mentioned in a list of pubs of 1761 but is not included in a list for 1792. The name suggests that it may have been used as a collecting and forwarding place for goods delivered by horse-drawn

*The **Wagon and Horses** was on the west side of Raven Lane.*

116

waggons. Before becoming an inn in 1619, it was the home of Mr. Edward Colbatch, shoemaker and a member of Ludlow Corporation. The richness of the external timbering on the front of the building was only revealed after refurbishment work in 1980. The wooden brackets depicting large busted ladies are supposed to be fertility symbols.

Opposite the **Wagon & Horses** at No. 7 Raven Lane was the **Prince of Wales** which was formerly called the **White Horse**. Town records show that in 1706, No. 7 and three other houses in Narrow Lane were left by Benjamin Careless, a Ludlow innholder, for the benefit of his children. Isaac Jones bought the property in 1807 and converted it into an inn, called at first the **White Horse** with Thomas Preece as innkeeper. In Jones' will of 1842 it was one of two properties left to his son Richard. Jones also left a messuage in High Street to his son Thomas and a leasehold messuage at the top of Broad Street to his daughter-in-law Mary. By 1859 the inn had been re-named the **Prince of Wales**.

Richard Jones was a bookseller and printer with a messuage, shop and printing office in Broad Street. In 1877 he left the messuage, shop and office to his son Henry, dividing the stock in trade among all his children, the messuage, including the inn now called the **Prince of Wales**, in Raven Lane to his son Whitmore, and a moiety (or half) of 13 cottages in Upper Gaolford to Mary Jane, wife of the testator's son Charles Richard and her children.

The inn had probably ceased trading by this time. At any rate, when it was sold to John Griffiths, mason, in 1879 it was no longer a public house, although apparently the pub interior remained for over a century until modernisation in the 1980s.

Other inns that at one time or another seem to have existed in Raven Lane include the **Plume of Feathers**, which is mentioned in a list of 1759; and the **Turk's Head**, listed in 1641, which may have been the same establishment as the **Saracen's Head**, recorded in a directory of 1822, but which by 1840 is no longer included. A **Saracen's Head** is mentioned in a poignant diary entry of 29 March 1828 by Mr. T. Griffith, a Ludlow printer and auctioneer, as follows: 'My father departed this life about 10 minutes before 4 in the afternoon. Taking inventory at the **Saracen's Head**'. Turk's Head is often a variant of Saracen's Head, whilst a Saracen, originally a nomad of the Arabian desert, came to mean Arab, then Moslem, especially in connection with the Crusades. Noble families, who had taken part in the Crusades, often chose to include a Saracen's head as part of their coat of arms. The head was then transferred to inn signs, and, of course, the Salwey family crest is a Saracen's head. Heads apparently abounded in Ludlow, and in addition to the Saracen there was supposed to be a **Goat's Head** in Raven Lane, but its whereabouts is unknown.

CHAPTER NINE

Old Street

Since Roman times and even earlier Old Street has been part of one of the main north—south routes along the Welsh border, with a ford across the River Teme eventually replaced by Ludford Bridge. The top end was renowned as one of the town's major markets—for pigs—while the bottom end, below Old Gate, was the site for the holding of circuses and fairs including May Day activities with its open-air dances.

Up to the 1930s the name Old Street only included the road as far as Old Gate, the section below the boundary walls being known as Oldgate Fee. This was a misnomer, however, because the name had nothing to do with Old Gate but referred to Holdgate Fee, the fee or rent due from the householders to the Lord of the Manor of Holdgate, in the Corvedale, who owned the land. According to a Ludlow handbook of 1865, this fee had never been collected since a day when 'the women assembled in a body and drove the collector out of the place with mops and broom-stails'.

Right at the top of Old Street on the corner with Bull Ring is a building housing the Olive Branch restaurant and two shops, which used to be an inn called the **Imperial Vaults**. Before that it was the **Bear and White Lion**, or variations of that name, and before that it was the **Prince Rupert Inn**, named after King Charles' cousin and one of the king's commanders who was often in Ludlow during the Civil War of 1642-46.

At the beginning of the 18th century the innkeeper and owner from at least 1724 until his death in 1729 was Rice Prickett. Appearing before a local court for 'keeping shuffle board tables' and for serving drink during divine service in 1727, Prickett died a wealthy man. He left possessions valued at £406 10s. 9d., a sizeable amount in

119

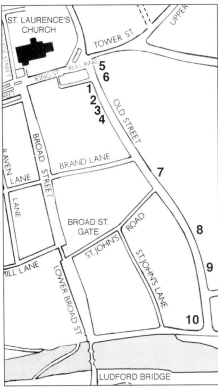

Old Street.

1—Imperial Vaults
2—Golden Lion
3—Castle Tavern
4—Green Dragon
5—Pheasant
6—Falcon
7—Friar's Inn
8—Hen and Chickens
9—Horse and Jockey *
10—Bay Horse
*—*Open in 2002*

those days, which despite reductions still left a total of £279 5s. 5d. The detailed inventory gives a good idea of what life at the inn must have been like in those days. The premises were timber-framed, probably dating from the mid-17th century and, backing onto Pepper Lane, had its own brewhouse which contained a brass furnace, mashing and watering tubs, coolers and other equipment. The stock in the cellar came to 549 gallons of ale and beer in hogsheads. Also stocked were cider, perry, rum, sherry, Canary and Rhenish wine. In the kitchen were eight spits for the roasting of meat and game, a toaster for cheese and a roaster for apples, together with a copper tea

*The **Prince Rupert**, the **Bear and White Lion**, and the **Imperial Vaults**—this building is now two shops and a restaurant.*

kettle and a tin coffee pot. In those days travellers ate in the kitchen unless they were 'quality'—that is coach passengers or people in private conveyances who would be served in a private room.

A lively description of an inn kitchen/dining room is given by Carl Philipp Moritz, who visited England in 1782:

> The chimney in this kitchen where they were roasting and boiling, seemed to be taken off from the rest of the room and enclosed by a wooden partition; the rest of the apartment was made use of as a sitting and eating room. All round the sides were shelves with pewter dishes and plates, and the ceiling was well stored with provisions of various kinds, such as sugar loaves, black puddings, hams, sausages, flitches of bacon, etc.

For the guests staying at the **Prince Rupert** there were chambers, often being both bedroom and sitting room, with 15 feather beds ranging from truckle bedsteads to one with 'blew hangings, rail and tester', while there were 42 pairs of sheets. There were also 12 chamber pots and 22 candlesticks. Nearly 50 pictures were displayed on the premises including one of Prince Rupert, although only valued at 1s. The most valuable single item of furniture was a clock and case worth £6. Provision would have been made for the stabling, feeding and harnessing of the guests' horses and Rice Prickett himself was something of a horse fancier.

A **White Lion** is mentioned in 1742 and a **White Lion and Bear** in 1782; by 1792 the inn had become the **Bear and White Lyon**, referring either to bear-baiting in the adjoining Bull Ring, or the heraldic sign of the earls of March and Edward IV. In 1822 it reverted to just being called the **White Lion**, but was soon back to the **Bear & White Lion**, when an auction sale was held in March 1826 of 'all the household goods & furniture, brewing utensils, casks of Mr. Charles Lucas, who is going to leave the same'. The items comprised:

> Tent bedsteads, & hangings, feather beds, bolster & pillows, blankets, & coverlets, oak dining & other tables, chairs, swing glasses, & wash-hand stands, fender & fire-irons, together with all the kitchen requisites & culinary goods, a quantity of hogsheads, half hogsheads & smaller barrels, trams, tunpails, coolers, mashing tubs etc., 80 gallon cast iron furnace, and a 30 gallon ditto (nearly new), malt mill, lot of sheep pens etc.

In 1840 the inn became the **Bear & Lion**, and by the 1880s it had become the **Imperial Vaults** selling wine and spirits and offering the game of billiards. Apart from its usual meaning of empire, an 'imperial' was a luggage trunk that had been adapted for stowing on the roof of a coach. In 1888 the licensee was William Hopkins, but in a licensing return of 1901 the inn was shown as being owned by Ind Coope & Co. with John Richards as occupier. There had been three changes of occupation or ownership in the previous five years. The return indicated that **Imperial Vaults** had a six-day full license held since about 1839 and that it consisted of a bar, smoke room, commercial room, billiard room and four bedrooms. The rateable value was given as £34.

It was soon after this that the inn was delicensed and the premises were taken over as offices by a family firm of auctioneers founded by William Norton. Mr. Norton was also founder-official of the Ludlow Electric Light Co. Ltd., and subsequently turned the **Vaults** into the Imperial Chambers as offices for the electricity company. It became the Olive Branch restaurant in the 1960s.

*The **Golden Lion** about the beginning of the 20th century.*

An antiques shop at No. 12 Old Street together with part of the adjoining Shropshire County Library was once the **Golden Lion** (a sign referring heraldically to Henry I)—one of the town's leading coaching inns in the 18th and 19th centuries. It was the starting point of one of the last two coaches to operate before the train took over, running to Birmingham. It is mentioned in a list of inns of 1792, and in 1806 it was described as being 'in the Pig Market'. Later a Regency façade, a rarity in Ludlow, was added to the building together with two large bow windows.

In 1840 the **Golden Lion**'s landlord, John Williams, was involved in local politics. He told a Select Committee on Ludlow Elections 'We have no Tories or Radicals, the politics of Ludlow are whether we are to choose a member for ourselves or have one family dictate to us ... and we are called Clivites and Reformers'.

Several auctions were held at the **Golden Lion** in the 1840s. In 1859 the innkeeper was Edward Halfhide and in 1888 it was Marianne Belson. In a directory of 1900 the **Golden Lion** was described as a commercial hotel and posting house with 'comfortably furnished rooms' and offering 'open or closed conveyances'. Frederick William Beeston, the proprietor, was also 'an ale and porter bottler, mineral water manufacturer and jobmaster'. In a licensing return a year later, the inn consisted of a bar, parlour, smoke room, commercial room, kitchen and seven bedrooms. There was stabling for seven horses. The owner and occupier was Hamelin James Rhys, the third change in five years. The rateable value was £21 5s. and its full licence had been granted about 1841.

By 1926 it had eschewed both licence and liquor and had become the Lion Temperance Hotel 'a reasonably priced and homely hotel with all modern conveniences and lock-up garages' with William Downs as proprietor. In the mid-1930s No. 12 became a cycle shop and the public library moved next door some 30 years ago. The wide brick arch indicating the drive-in to the back yard has now been converted into a shop window. The stables at the rear were demolished, an old well was filled in with rubble,

*The **Golden Lion** is now an antiques shop.*

*28 Old Street, once the **Castle Tavern**.*

and two houses were built in their place. The original sign bracket still hangs above the front door, having been brought back after gracing another antiques shop in Broad Street for a while. Underneath No. 12 is a cellar which was used as an air-raid shelter during the last war.

At No. 28 Old Street, now a private house, was once the **Castle Tavern**, which until the 1850s was known as the **White Hart**. The name originally came from Richard II's heraldic symbol, but later it came to be the generic term for a tavern. A **White Hart** in Ludlow is first mentioned in 1742 and again in 1840, but an 1859 directory includes it as the **Castle Inn** with John Boden as licensee. In 1888 the owner and occupier was Emily Reynolds Harding, who

*The **Green Dragon** in 2001.*

was also described as a 'shoeing and general smith'. By 1901 Emily was still resident, but was then called Rawlings, having married, and the tavern, as it was referred to, is described as having a bar, tap room, parlour, back kitchen and six bedrooms. There was stabling for two horses. The rateable value was assessed at only £18 and the nature of trade described as 'agricultural'.

During the First World War the **Tavern** was run by 44-year-old John Lamsdell, married with two children.

At the time of May Fair in 1916, hearing that a fire had broken out in the furniture warehouse of Bodenhams at the rear of 59 Broad Street, he went to help—the fire brigade being hard-pressed with so many young men away at war. A floor collapsed, slightly injuring three firemen, but next day Mr. Lamsdell's body was found under a ton of debris and piled up carpets. After this tragedy the **Castle Tavern** closed and became a private residence.

A handsome new sign on the front of nearby Mortimer Court and a mural on the passage wall leading to the rear are clear indicators that the premises once housed a former public house called the **Green Dragon.** The name is apparently not connected with St. George and the Dragon but rather is taken from the coat of arms of the earls of Pembroke. The **Green Dragon** first appears in a list of inns for 1742 and again in 1792. In 1822 a poster advertised the sale of the contents of the inn.

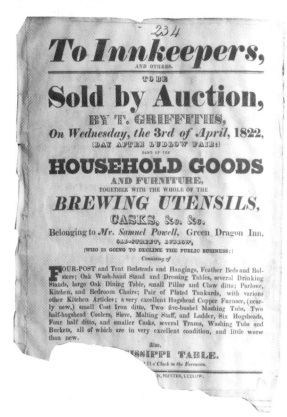

*The 1822 sale at the **Green Dragon**.*

In 1888 the licensed victualler, Theophilus Hodges, was also head agent for the Liverpool, Victoria Legal Assurance Office in Old Street.

The **Green Dragon** was the type of pub that had been common in Ludlow. Two steps led up to an ordinary house door and then into surprisingly spacious quarters. In the licensing return of 1901, the inn is reported to comprise a bar, parlour, two kitchens and seven bedrooms with stables for four horses. The owner and occupier was Eliza Hodges, who had taken over in the previous five

*The shops at the top of Old Street which, in conjunction with the Turner Street frontage, once formed the **Pheasant***

years. The full licence dated from about 1839 and the rateable value was £19 10s.

In 1926 the landlord was Frederick Peake, who was also the brewer of the beer he retailed. It must have been appreciated for he was still there in 1941. The inn was still going strong in the 1950s with the wooden casks kept on a stillion and the beer drawn direct into glasses in traditional fashion, but sadly it was closed by the brewery during Easter 1954. They also owned the **Hen & Chickens** across the road and decided that one had to go—the latter apparently being the better proposition.

On the eastern side of Old Street at the northern end with the corner of Tower Street once stood the **Pheasant Inn**. It occupied an ancient site which once consisted of 'a corner shop with solar over and cellar under', and a complex of four 'shops with solars over'. Solar was the name given to private living rooms above a shop where the family could be 'alone'. In the middle was a small internal courtyard. These properties were owned by the Palmers' Guild who let them out.

Many taverns of 15th-century Ludlow were in cellars and the vaulted cellar at No. 1 Old Street probably would have sold wine. Customers were no doubt served by a tapster like drunken 'Simon the Cellarer' as illustrated in the misericord in St. Laurence's parish church. With the demise of the Palmers' Guild, this and other properties in Ludlow were taken over by the Corporation, who leased the Old Street building to tenants for £1 *per annum*.

The **Pheasant** came into existence in the 17th century. There are references to two of the landlords in probate inventories taken in the latter part of that century. Thomas Evans, described as victualler, left an inventory in 1669 valued at £196 13s. 4d., while Richard Coney, innkeeper, was valued at £126 7s. 6d. in 1677.

In 1790 the innkeeper was given as Levy Penfor and in 1827 it was a Mr. Coxhales, who appeared to be in some financial trouble. An inventory of his goods was made 'under an execution' and there was a sale of his cows on the Bull Ring. In 1829 an inquest was held on a man who 'died at the

*Once the **Falcon** in Old Street.*

Pheasant from drinking spirits'. In 1885 the licence of the **Pheasant Inn** was transferred from Edward Brownell to Thomas Sheldon. Sheldon was also described as a gunsmith in 1888 and was to be the last landlord, for the pub closed soon after the end of the First World War. The much changed building became a grocers' shop and now houses the Shapla Tandoori Restaurant and Stag Leisurewear. The cellar, barrel-vaulted and as big as a crypt, was used as an air-raid shelter during the Second World War, but was filled in in 1963.

Nearby, at No. 5, stood the **Falcon Inn**. In 1626 it was mentioned in the list of only 16 inns in Ludlow known by their sign—it was then the town's first **Red Lion**. It was later known as the **Seven Stars**, before becoming the **Falcon**.

A probate inventory of Francis Clent, Junior, described as a 'haberdasher', who was buried on 17 December 1662 aged only 21, shows that he shared the same premises as his father, who was landlord of the **Red Lion**. The building, which was described as a large inn with an entrance in Tower Street, became a spacious town house with a brick front, behind which apparently the richly moulded ceiling beams of the former inn could still be seen. It is now a shop.

Old Gate, which was half-way down the street, used to have twin drum towers on each side of the road, similar to those still existing at Broad Gate. The 13th-century gate, originally part of the town's defences, was mainly used for the collection of tolls. One of the stone towers—where No. 87, a brick building, presently stands—housed a tavern called at various times the **Old Gate**, the **Drum**, the **Mug House**, the **Dog**, and the **Tap House**. Mug House was a 17th-century term for an ale-house, mug being used in the sense of a pot or ewer.

William Waldron was innkeeper of the **Mug House** in 1790. A benefit society called the Mughouse Society held meetings here or at the **Golden Cross**, as is shown in 1817 when the tenant of a shop in Shoemakers' Row mortgaged the shop to the trustees of this society. By 1822 it was called the **Dog**. In her reminiscences between 1809 and 1830, Ludlow's oldest inhabitant, Mary Jones, wrote:

> I remember on the site of Friar's Terrace, in Old Street, an old round tower, the remains of the Old Gate. It formed part of an inn known as the **Mug House**, afterwards the **Dog**, at the back of the premises being a cock pit. I have many times from an upper window looked down to this pit to see battles fought. Thirteen of these battles were called a 'main'.
>
> Opposite this tavern, and adjoining the Workhouse entrance, were the parish stocks, often occupied by drunkards. [The drunkards and petty offenders were confined by the wrists and ankles between two stakes or stocks on either side.]
>
> These stocks were afterwards removed to the Market Hall. At the back of the Workhouse was the House of Correction.

After 1837 the Workhouse and House of Correction were known as Lane's Asylum and were used as almshouses.

The sport of cock-fighting, introduced into Britain by the Romans and much favoured by monarchs such as Henry VIII and James I, went on at many Ludlow inns including the **Mug House** and the **Feathers** until 1849, when it 'died a natural and generally unlamented death'. The cockpit, where the game-cocks fought, was usually paved with sheep knuckle bones to give the birds a non-skid foothold. Battle Royals (a number of birds left to fight until

LUDLOW.

TO BE

SOLD BY AUCTION,

BY T. GRIFFITHS,

At the Elephant and Castle Inn, in Ludlow,

On MONDAY, the 13th Day of DECEMBER, next,

Between the Hours of 4 and 6 o'clock in the Afternoon,

Subject to Conditions of Sale to be then Produced.

(Unless disposed of in the mean time by private Contract, of which Notice will be given :)

A FREEHOLD

MESSUAGE,

OR

Dwelling House and Garden,

CALLED THE HORN & TRUMPET INN,

AND ALSO,

Two Cottages, or Tenements with a Garden attached to one of them, and a large Barn or Building,
adjoining together, and under one Roof, situate
in Old Gate's-fee, in or near the Town of LUD-
LOW, and now in the Possession of Mr. JOHN
CHARLTON, and his Tenants.

The Barn or Building is 14 feet wide or thereabout, and 22 feet
long, with a Tiled Roof, and is capable of being converted into a
Dwelling House or Workshop, at an easy expence. --- The Premises are
in tenantable repair, and are well supplied with good Spring Water.

☞ *For further particulars, and to treat for the same, apply to*
Mr. *LLOYD, Solicitor, LUDLOW.*

?low, 2nd. November, 1824.

Printed at the Office of T. Griffiths, Bull-Ring.

Sale of the **Horn and Trumpet** *in 1824.*

129

there was one survivor) and Welsh Mains (where eight pairs were matched, then the eight winners until only one bird was left alive) were held. Wakes (a name which became attached to annual fairs) were often the occasion for cock-fighting. In the days when servants took holidays to attend a 'cocking', it was natural that such affairs should be arranged for a general holiday season, like a wake. The Shropshire newspapers in the latter part of the

*The **Hen and Chickens** is now a guest house.*

18th century contained many advertisements of 'cockings' for high stakes, as much as 10 guineas a battle and 200 guineas the main.

Later, the inn was re-named yet again as **Friars Inn**, standing on the northern side of Friars Walk. In 1859 the landlord was John Hancocks, but it closed in the 1880s.

Now a well respected guest house, the **Hen and Chickens** at No. 103 was for long a public house, but once again under a variety of names. It may have been the **Horn & Trumpet** of Old Gate Fee mentioned in 1795 and put up for sale by auction in December 1824 at the **Elephant & Castle Inn**.

By 1844 it had become the **Hen & Chickens**, with Timothy and Thomas Meyrick as licensees. However, in 1851 it had gained a new, if temporary, name—the **Railway Arms**. This was probably because the wasteland at the back of the pub was used to store all the heavy material needed for the building of the railway from Shrewsbury to Hereford, and railway navvies had big thirsts. The Shrewsbury to Ludlow section opened on 20 April 1852, but the connection to

Hereford was not completed until December 1853. Shortly afterwards it became the **Hen & Chickens** once again.

In 1888 the landlord was Joseph Ovens, about which time it was described as a 'singing pub', being a focal point for local residents with leagues for darts and dominoes. In 1900 it was run by Frederick William Willstrop, who was also described as a 'hairdresser'. By 1901 the inn was owned by Ind Coope & Co. with Frederick St. Willstrop as licensee. With a rateable value of £19 and a full license going back to 1840, it comprised a bar, kitchen, taproom, sitting-room and five bedrooms. There was stabling for four horses. It was noted that there had been two landlords in the previous five years. In 1892 a case against a previous landlord for selling adulterated gin was dismissed. Thomas Innes Watkins was the licensee in 1926 and Sidney Edwards in 1941. The last licensees were Mr. and Mrs. Halford, who sold the establishment in December 1998, after which the premises were converted to a guest house by the present owners.

There are several different versions of the meaning of this unusual name. Before the 17th century a hen and chickens were symbolic in Christian art of God's providence. By the 17th century it was used to describe the Pleiades, the group of stars in the constellation Taurus. A century later it was used to name a compound daisy, such as London Pride, but by the late 19th century the expression was applied to a children's game. A grey hen was the name given to a stone bottle for holding liquor, and large and small pewter pots mixed together were often called 'hen and chickens'. Another hen expression was tappit-hen, a Scottish term, used for a large beer or wine measure; also a lidded pewter drinking vessel with a handle, and having a slim neck and broad body resembling a hen.

The only inn still in existence in Old Street is the **Horse & Jockey** at No. 113. This is again another example of an inn which underwent several name changes. It was probably first called the **Hunting Horse**, becoming the **Mare & Groom** in 1749, the **Horse & Groom** in 1750, and finally the **Horse & Jockey** in 1757.

Above the main door, engraved in glass, is the name of Edward Sheldon, the most illustrious of over half a century of Sheldons who ran the inn. When the **Crown & Horseshoes** in Lower Broad Street closed in 1878 its landlord, Thomas Sheldon, who also described

himself as a blacksmith, took up the licence of the **Horse & Jockey** and a Sheldon remained there for some 60 years. His son, Edward, eventually took over as owner and occupier and ran the inn with his wife Elizabeth, brewing his own beer. He was there in 1901 when a licensing inspection was carried out. This showed that the inn consisted of a bar, taproom, smokeroom, kitchen, parlour and five bedrooms. There was stabling for 11 horses. The rateable value for this free house was £24 and its full licence had been held since 1840.

Edward Sheldon went on to carve out a distinquished civic career and was Mayor of Ludlow on two separate occasions from 1902 to 1904 and from 1917 to 1921. He was still at the **Horse & Jockey** in 1926. At Christmas time he would treat the local children to 'tanners', the old sixpence, which he would throw into the street, after first making them red hot on the stove! The family seemed to specialise in running inns, for in 1900 there was a Thomas Sheldon at the **Pheasant**

*The **Horse and Jockey** Bowling Club in the 1930s.*

*The **Horse and Jockey** in 2002.*

in Old Street whilst John Sheldon was landlord of the **Barley Mow** in Lower Broad Street. By 1941 the landlord of the **Horse & Jockey** was Cecil W.F. Morgan and the Sheldon dynasty had come to an end.

Parts of the **Horse & Jockey** were apparently at one time also within the boundaries of the county of Herefordshire, making one landlord claim: 'if you put your feet inside the pub you couldn't be arrested by the police'—this, at a time when each county had its own police force.

Alan and Kath Walker ran the inn from 1974 to 1996. One link from the past was the Pigeon Club which continued for a while and then stopped. At the beginning of the 21st century, the **Horse & Jockey** is a managed Marston-owned pub, but the Edward Sheldon sign is still above the main entrance.

Before a housing estate called Jockey Fields was built at the back of the **Horse & Jockey** about 25 years ago the area used to be a focal point of social activity. As well as a bowling green and club, small circuses and fairground rides were held there while waiting to proceed to the town centre for fairs.

May day dances were held to a surprisingly late period in Ludlow. A maypole used to be 'reared' on a particular spot in Old Gate Fee, on the road south of the Old Gate. The last one was erected in 1864 and stayed there until it decayed away in 1876. The May-day celebrations were then taken under the patronage of a publican and for many years a maypole stood in the yard of a nearby public house, probably the **Horse & Jockey**. It was decorated yearly with tinsel paper and garlands. Sports practised included old women's races for pounds of tea and grinning for packets of snuff. Up to 20 fiddlers played at the open-air dances and dancing couples used the whole length of the street.

*The **Bay Horse** is now a private house.*

Circuses must have been exotic affairs in those days. For instance in October 1842, 'Van Amburgh's royal collection of trained lions, tigers, leopards etc' were exhibited in a marquee in Old Gate Fee. This was followed by a procession of eight cream-coloured horses through Old Gate Fee into the Bull Ring, then along High Street and into Castle Street. Another time there were 46 grey and cream horses together with a giraffe and an elephant. In April 1844, came Richard Sands' American Circus, with a number of American Equestrians and 40 highly trained American horses who performed in Mr. Powell's meadow in Old Gate Fee. A grand procession followed together with a brass band.

Even more bizarre was an earlier show in 1841, actually sponsored by the Licensed Victuallers of Ludlow—a one-day show including a 'Miraculous Menagerie with flying rabbits and guinea pigs; transformation of vegetables into lozenges; and enchanted fruit'. The event concluded with the 'Great Gun Delusion'. The admission price was 2s. for boxes and 6d. for the gallery.

At the bottom of Old Street near the bank of the Teme, once stood the **Bay Horse**. It is recorded that for Edward VII's coronation in 1901 a tour of Ludlow's boundaries was made including a trip by the Mayor in a rowing boat from Corve Bridge, under Dinham and Ludford bridges, and 'still onwards [to] the Bay Horse ferry (where the crew will be supplied with refreshments by the Aldermen of the District)'. A boat continued to ferry people across the Teme at a spot where the river was fordable until well into the 20th century. A concrete wall and sewers now prevent access to the Teme. The **Bay Horse** itself closed, became a lodging house and then a base for a taxi firm. It is now a private residence called Riverside.

CHAPTER TEN

Corve Street

With the gradual demise of the glove-making industry due to competition from abroad, malting, the ancient art of converting barley into malt came to be Ludlow's most important manufacturing trade. In 1822 Ludlow was described as a town where gloves and malting 'contribute the principal manufacture', but by 1859 glove-making was extinct. The hub for the malting business was Corve Street. The town hosted 18 malting businesses in 1770, a number which had increased to 30 in 1828; in 1841 there were 13 malsters in Corve Street alone. Malsters must have been well regarded in local circles for Thomas Pritchard, one of the Corve Street malsters, was appointed Treasurer of Ludlow Council at £25 a year in 1836. An example of a malthouse and kiln still survives at the rear of No. 139a Corve Street, since used for other purposes and now in somewhat forlorn condition.

To add to the colourful nature of this long street, which was the main route north towards Shrewsbury, were poultry and sheep near the Bull Ring on market days, the plying of carriers' carts bringing produce and people into town, a brewery, and of course numerous inns and taverns.

The old town wall marks the dividing line between the Bull Ring and Corve Street, where there used to stand the impressive gates with twin drum towers on either side. Abutting the external west side of the remaining part of the gatehouse at No. 1 is the **Compasses**, which is situated on a medieval site and is one of the town's earliest inns. Like most of the properties in Corve Street, the inn was destroyed during the Civil War. Afterwards the Corporation gave priority to replacing burnt houses with incentives

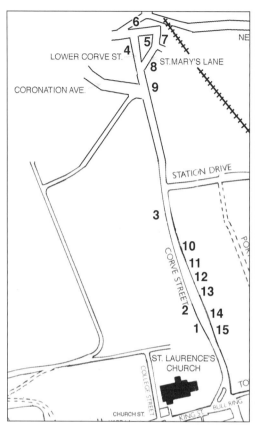

Corve Street.

for quick rebuilding. Thus in 1649 John Cleobury was granted the property which is now the **Compasses** with 'no fine but to build'. Some of the original beams still stood and were incorporated into the new inn.

For many years it was actually known as the **Three Compasses** (the name is usually a reference to the compass(es) that appear on the arms of the guilds: one for masons, two for joiners, and three for carpenters). It appears in a list of inns in 1742 and again in 1792, but soon after the latter date, when the victualler was Stephen Pinches, the 'Three' was dropped.

A poster appeared in 1820 stating: 'Stolen three ewes and six lambs from Old Field, near Ludlow. Information and half guinea reward to Mr. Hotchkiss, **Compasses Inn**, Ludlow or three guineas, if stolen, and convicted of offence'. In 1822 it was named as one of Ludlow's principal inns. Mr. Hotchkiss died in 1827 followed two years later by Mrs. Hotchkiss. In 1859 the landlord was John Pearce.

In 1880 the **Compasses** was put up for sale by auction when it was described as follows:

Containing on ground floor—2 kitchens, billiard room,
well fitted bar and market room;
On first floor—large club room and 3 good bedrooms.
On second floor—4 good sized bedrooms;
and in basement some capital dry cellaring.
The out-offices are very commodious—stabling for 30 horses,
lock-up coach house, shedding and good piggeries.

A further notice of particulars stated that the reserve of £1,500 had not been met, and the **Compasses** had been withdrawn at £1,425. However, it was sold immediately afterwards to William Allum for £1,450. The particulars also pointed out that it was: 'an estate in Ludlow belonging to the Earl of Powis and Lord Windsor [comprising the **Compasses** and 2 houses in Corve Street and 6 houses in Bell Lane]'. William Allum was still running the inn in 1888.

The inn was one of the town's major centres for carriers' carts. In the 1830s vans and carts, laden with goods and people, loaded and put down at the inn from Bishop's Castle and other neighbouring villages,

*The **Compasses** hides behind the adjoining building and
benefits from the wide pavement.*

while in 1885 it had seven departures a week to provide a regular service to outlying areas. In 1900 carriers called at the **Compasses** from the following villages: Bouldon, Brand Hill, Clee St. Margaret, Downton Castle, Hayton, Hope Bagot, Stanton Lacy and Sutton Hill.

Allum's widow, Alice Mary, was the owner and occupier of the **Compasses** when a licensing inspection was carried out in 1901. The inn, which had had a full licence since 1848, was described as a 'good market house, agricultural, in the town', and comprised a bar, two parlours, market room, kitchen and six bedrooms. Good, clean stabling was provided for 10 horses. In 1892, a fine of 1s. with costs of 8s. had been imposed for selling adulterated whisky, but not against the present occupier and the licence was not endorsed. By 1926 Benjamin Harding was landlord, when he was described as a 'brewer of beer retailed', and in 1941, the licensee was given as Archibald Webb, who was also listed as 'beer retailer only'.

Farmers' wives used to sell their poultry from pens set up on the wide pavement in front of the **Compasses** until the early part of the 20th century.

A special meeting of the Ludlow Licensed Victuallers Association was held at the **Compasses** on 5 May 1942 to arrange new drink

9 Corve Street, once the ***Green Dragon***.

prices. These included whisky and gin at 1s. 3d., draft beer (mild) at 11d. per pint and draft beer (bitter) at 1s. 1d.

In 1951 the *Ludlow Advertiser* reported that workmen carrying out structural repairs to the inn uncovered a well, 20ft. deep and containing 12ft. of water, under a paving stone. The well digger's initials and the date of construction 'W.E., 1639' were contained in an inscription on a stone on the well lip.

In 1982 the inn was again in the news with the *Ludlow Advertiser* reporting that the then licensee, Peter Crowley, had discovered the previous year a hidden room during rewiring and wood treatment work of the living quarters. Amongst the rubble were found four human thigh and other bones.

Shortly afterwards the inn was taken over by Pubmaster, and over the years various changes have been carried out resulting in the stables and passage way being incorporated into the main building. Still visible is a massive beam running across the roof pierced with iron hooks and pegs from which stable tack used to hang.

No. 9 is now a solicitor's office, but was once the original **Green Dragon**, one of at least two in Corve Street alone. Although

This restaurant was once the
Eagle and Child.

Corve Street took a real battering during the Civil War, with the Royalist troops demolishing properties to obtain a clear field of fire from the town walls and to ensure the Parliamentarians could not plant explosives, they seemed to have had their priorities right because they allowed three buildings to survive between Corve Gate and St. Leonard's churchyard—all of them inns. They were the **Green Dragon** at No. 9, the **Talbot** at No. 139 and the **Rose & Crown** at No. 145. A **Green Dragon**, mentioned in 1619, may have been this one, and is listed again in 1626 when it was one of 16 inns to be recognised by its sign. A **Green Dragon** is mentioned in 1742; two are listed in 1790, and again in 1792, one of which was definitely in Corve Street.

A few doors further down is No. 17, which is now a Michelin rated restaurant called the Hibiscus, but which used to be the **Eagle** or the **Eagle and Child**—an inn since the 17th century. The eagle was a Christian and heraldic symbol and the emblem on Roman military standards, but the Eagle and Child on pub signs was usually a reference to the Stanleys, earls of Derby. Sir Thomas Latham, one of the family's ancestors in the 14th century, had an illegitimate son, which he had placed under a tree in which an eagle had built its nest. He then took his wife for a walk round the estate and they 'discovered' the infant. Sir Thomas persuaded his wife that they should adopt it.

However, in this case there was probably a more prosaic reason, although a good one—one of the landlords had the surname Child. This was Henry Child, who was the landlord of the **Eagle** towards the end of the 17th century. He was described as a 'cooper' for his probate inventory in 1685, which was valued at £110 4s. 6d. His widow Joan Child had a probate inventory of £368 or £338 after debts and property leases had been deducted in 1704. This inventory also showed that the **Eagle and Child** inn had named chambers for guests, two parlours and £75 worth of 'ale and beer'. Various entertainments used to be held there including cock-fighting. One such event in 1731 was billed as the 'Great Cock Match'.

A painting of Corve Street in 1812 by William Gwynn (1782-1860), the Ludlow artist, includes a timber-framed **Eagle and Child** tavern. The inn, which was subsequently refaced in brick, consisted of a bar, kitchen, clubroom, sitting-room, and four bedrooms.

In June 1840 the Ludlow Conservative Association held a meeting at Mr. Walter Owen's **Eagle Inn**, when members were requested to meet punctually at 8 o'clock. In 1859 the landlord was given as Edward Edwards and James Jones was licensed victualler in 1888. The inn, which had stabling for nine horses, was also another carriers' calling point with carts going to five villages, namely Burley, Clee St. Margaret, Hayton, Hayton's Bent, and Sutton Hill. In 1898 the landlord was fined 20s. with costs of 10s. for permitting drunkenness on the premises.

By the turn of the century the inn was owned by Ind Coope & Co. with George Holt as licensee. Later landlords included Herbert Bailey in 1926 and John Taylor in 1941. It closed as a pub about 1955 and became a licensed restaurant, originally known as the Eagle House, then the Oaks, and, by the turn of the century, the Hibiscus. Medieval burgage plots at the rear have been turned into a car park. A financial company next door, at No.18/20, which was probably once part of the **Eagle and Child,** keeps the association with the name Eagle House.

Unusually for Ludlow, there seems to be a big gap before the next inn. It is after the junction with Coronation Avenue that the **Unicorn** is reached at No. 66 in Lower Corve Street. At one time, though, one did

140

BOROUGH OF LUDLOW.

OLD ESTABLISHED INN,
AND OTHER VALUABLE

FREEHOLD PROPERTY.

To be Sold by Auction,

BY T. GRIFFITHS,

At the UNICORN INN, Corve Street, Ludlow,
On **THURSDAY**, *the 3rd. Day of* **JUNE**, 1841,
AT SIX o'CLOCK IN THE AFTERNOON.

Together, or in such Lots as shall be agreed upon at the time of Sale, and Subject to Conditions to be then produced.

ALL THAT OLD

Established & well accustomed Inn,
CALLED THE

UNICORN

Situate in *Corve Street*, in the Borough of *Ludlow*, now in the Possession of
Mr. HENRY OLIVER.

ALSO, ALL THOSE TWO GOOD

DWELLING HOUSES,

Adjoining therto, now in the Possession of RICHARD FRANCIS and WILLIAM
WARMAN, together with the TAN YARD behind the same; having a Frontage
of about 84 feet, and a Depth of near 90 feet to the River Corve, by which the
Property is bounded on the West. ALSO a good new built double Stall Stable,
situate in *Saint Mary's Lane*, and now occupied by Mr. OLIVER with the Unicorn
Inn.

The *Unicorn* is very conveniently situated for an Inn and has had great Custom for many Years,
and it would with the Houses and Tan Yard adjoining, form an excellent Site for a Brewery, or a
Woollen or other Manufactory.

The respective Tenants will shew the Premises, and for further particulars apply to Messrs. WILLIAMS
and URWICK, Solicitors, Ludlow.

Ludlow, May 14th. 1841.

LUDLOW: PRINTED BY T. GRIFFITHS, AGENT TO THE SUN FIRE OFFICE.

*Sale of the **Unicorn** in 1841.*

have to pass the Ludlow and Craven Arms Brewery at Nos. 45 to 48,
which operated from 1895 to the early 1930s from a former builders
yard. No. 45 and the rest of the brewery complex was demolished to
make way for the building of New Bromfield Road, now called
Coronation Avenue. Nos. 46, 47 and 48 were converted into the present
black and white houses on the corner.

The **Unicorn,** which might itself have become a brewery, dates
from the first half of the 17th century when this area, backing onto the

Corve river, was developed. Its name was derived from the heraldic use of the legendary animal. When James VI of Scotland became James I of England, one of the two unicorns on his Scottish royal arms displaced the Welsh dragon on the English royal arms, the other supporter being the lion. A unicorn also features on the arms of various Worshipful Companies.

One of the first recorded innholders in the 18th century was a woman, Blanche Styche, followed by William Powis who in 1750 left a probate inventory valued at £19 12s. Another landlady was a Mrs. Evans, who died in 1827. The inn is also mentioned in lists of licensed houses for 1792 and 1822. In June 1841 the **Unicorn**, described as that 'old established and well accustomed inn' and other valuable freehold property was to be sold by auction.

Although it was described as being suitable for a brewery or woolen manufactury, it remained an inn and in 1876 an inquest into the death of a child in bizarre circumstances was held there. Two men, lodgers of the house of Mr. Spotton, near the **Unicorn**, were in the street 'larking', one of them with a rose in his hand dosed with pepper following the other in order to place it to his nose. One of the men stumbled and fell backwards. A child of Mr. Spotton, three years old, was stood behind and was 'knocked down by the fall and seriously injured' and later died.

*The **Unicorn** sign.*

In a directory of 1888 Elizabeth Corfield was listed as both licensed victualler and brewer. During the Return of Licensed Houses for 1901 the **Unicorn**, which had a rateable value of £19 10s., was described as having a bar, parlour, kitchen and five bedrooms. Stabling, for four horses, required repairs and whitewashing. The owners were given as Elizabeth and Louisa Evans with William Herbert Evans as the occupier. A charge had been brought against a previous occupier in June 1892 for selling adulterated whisky when costs

*The **Unicorn** still flourishes in 2002.*

of 9s. 6d. were ordered to be paid together with 10s. 6d., as part of the analyst's fee.

The River Corve regularly burst its banks and Lower Corve Street was subject to flooding. After the great flood of 1885 a postcard was produced showing men sitting around a table in the bar of the **Unicorn** while flood water lapped the doorway. They had full pint pots of beer in front of them. Another postcard, of 1924, shows a flooded Lower Corve Street, still the main road out of Ludlow to Shrewsbury, after a thunderstorm. Before the river was dredged, houses on the east side of the street were often flooded and it wasn't unusual for empty barrels from the **Unicorn**'s cellar to float away. In 1900, the **Unicorn** was the base for a carrier operating to the village of Vernolds Common. In 1926 the landlord was still William Herbert Evans, but by 1941 Mrs. Violet Mary Gittins was in charge. The inn, a low, attractive timber-framed building, once sported a night club called Cagney's, but this apparently did not meet with Ludlow's requirements and the club was converted into a dining area, which is still the case today.

By Ludlow's standards the **Bridge Inn** at No. 77 by Corve Bridge is relatively new, being only 160 years old. Originally the **Queen's Arms**, after Queen Victoria, it was built in the 1840s by a local family called Bird who remained the licensees after selling it to Ind Coope & Co. Before the railway was built, the New Road turnpike up Gravel Hill passed to the right of the inn, which occupies an island site, and the road to Fishmoor went to the left. The landlord, Richard Bird, operated a haulage and removals business and the inn itself was used to store ricks of bark for the local tanneries which proliferated in Lower Corve Street.

On Guy Fawkes' night, a bonfire procession would start from the **Queen's Arms**:

> The procession of men and boys walking two by two, and carrying lighted torches, set out headed by a drum and fife band playing some lively tune such as Shrewsbury Quarry and marched through the Bull Ring, over Ludford Bridge up to Whitcliffe Hill, the appointed site of the bonfire. The 'guy', with a pipe in his mouth and a turnip lantern in his hand, was borne in a chair by four men in the midst of the procession, and duly burnt on the bonfire. Sometimes people created a nuisance by letting off fireworks along the route, but usually the police did not interfere unless there was an 'absolute necessity'.

By 1888 William, the son of Richard Bird, had taken over and was described as a 'licensed victualler, furniture remover, farmer and haulier'. The entry for the 1900 *Kelly's Directory* states: 'Bird, William, furniture remover and proprietor of the **Queen's Arms** commercial inn; goods removed in town or country on reasonable terms'. It was also a posting house with 'good bed and stabling accommodation'. A year later the inn, described as being on the outskirts of town with a rateable value of £50, consisted of a bar, parlour, two kitchens, and seven bedrooms. There was room for 14 horses, but the stabling was in need of whitewashing.

William Bird's mug, complete with his date of birth.

'A soldier and his family'.

William Bird issued a copper token at the turn of the century which could be exchanged for beer to the value of three pennies; one face of the token was decorated with hops. By 1926 the landlord was George Holloway and in 1941 it was Ernest Thomas Ralphs, who was also the motor engineer at Bridge Garage.

The name changed to the **Bridge Inn** in 1970 apparently to avoid confusion with the **Queen's Head** in Lower Galdeford. Now owned by Pubmaster, there is a poignant photograph hanging in the bar dated 1915 and titled 'A soldier and his family'. The caption reads: 'Thomas and Mary Lowe of the **Queen's Arms** (now the **Bridge**) in Lower Corve Street, with their five children, one of whom, William, had enlisted in the King's Shropshire Light Infantry. He later fought at Ypres but did [not] survive the war. In 1915, the county was gripped with patriotic fervour and families though apprehensive were proud of those who volunteered. Lent by Pat Perry, whose mother Frances Snow (née

*The **Bridge Inn** now.*

145

Lowe) is second from left'. A descendant of the Bird family, living nearby, still has in his possession a commemorative mug with the words: 'William Bird, **Queen's Arms**, Born Feb 19 1840'.

Across the road from the **Bridge Inn** was the **Mitre**, a sign which has been used for inns since the 15th century. It is a reference to the deeply cleft hat, having the shape of a pointed arch at the front and back, worn by bishops and some abbots. The inn, which was in Stanton Lacy parish, is mentioned in a list of licensed houses of 1822. The winter of 1829 was severe with heavy snow falling before Christmas. Four days afterwards a boy was drowned near the **Mitre** 'from sliding' presumably on the River Corve.

An annual 'Processioning Day' in which Ludlow schoolboys, accompanied by a clergyman, perambulated the town boundaries, had a connection with the **Mitre**. One boy, who took part in the perambulation between the years 1835 and 1840, later recalled:

> The old beadle led the way, preceding the Rector of the parish, and followed by the parish constable, who carried a ladder; then the boys from the schools of the town, two by two, each carrying a birch rod. It was good fun. We scrambled over the walls, walked through the boundary-houses, and at the **Mitre** Inn, at the extremity of Corve Street, there stood a porch with two side-holes through which we boys all went. Afterwards we had a jolly fight with our rods. If the old Rector could not go, he read prayers in Church and despatched us with his blessing.

The holes in the porch, it is thought, may once have been regarded as a sort of 'Needle's Eye' to be crept through 'for luck'.

In 1859 the landlord was given as Robert Allum. It is also recorded that in 1861 four carriers and a waggoner 'on travel' stayed at the **Mitre** and that a pigeon shooting match was held there in 1863.

*The **Mitre** in 2001 is now flats and an antiques shop.*

A picture of the railway at Ludlow, painted by William Gwynn, a local artist, shows the **Queen's Arms**, with one of the landlord's wagons in front, and the **Mitre Inn**, with its complex of outbuildings.

By the 1870s the **Mitre** had closed and for some years it was used by a firm of hauliers called Davies for their horse-drawn timber wagons and later steam wagons. About 30 years ago the building, now called Mitre House, was converted into flats and an antiques shop.

Returning towards the town centre on the eastern side of Corve Street one comes to St. Mary's Lane, which turns back on itself to Bromfield Road. At the end, where the lane joins the road leading to the **Bridge Inn**, is No. 11, now a private residence, but which was the **Cross Keys**, a beer house used by men working on the railway. The men also bought buckets of beer from the **Cross Keys** and hauled them up the embankment to the railway sidings where they worked.

In 1888 the innkeeper was William Price and in 1891 the inn was bought by Ind Coope & Co. with Robert Cooper as occupier and beer retailer. A case was brought against Cooper that year for supplying drink

*The **Cross Keys** is now a private house.*

147

during prohibited hours, but was dismissed. Ownership and occupant remained the same in 1901 when the rateable value was given as a modest £12 15s. for premises, which were in good condition and clean, consisting of just a bar, kitchen and four bedrooms.

Ludlow police, in the form of Superintendent Perry, objected when an application for the renewal of its licence was made in 1911 by the tenant Mr. Crowther. Superintendent Perry said the urinal and WC was in a yard on the opposite side of the street and appeared to be used by the family and customers. In his opinion every public house should be fitted up with a WC for the family and a separate one for the customers; he thought that sharing it was objectionable. There was a shed which could be used as a stable. Within 700 yards there were 12 other fully licensed houses and within 173 yards there were three, the nearest one being the **Queen's Arms**, 48 yards away. The other houses had equal if not better accommodation for people, horses and vehicles and were fully licensed, whilst this was a beer house which did but small trade. The landlord's stepson said the average weekly takings were £7 and trade was increasing, the inn being used by men working on the railway to take their meals in. A provisional licence was granted.

The **Cross Keys** (a common sign in Christian heraldry, but sometimes the trademark of a brewery) continued to trade until after the end of the Great War, but closed because of an 'on the slate' dispute. Some say the railwaymen caught the landlord adding extra chalk marks to the slate; others that they ran up such large unpaid bills that he was driven out of business.

Opposite the former Ludlow Brewery, at No. 98 Corve Street, was once another **Green Dragon,** which had been an inn for at least 300 years, but which lost its licence in the purge of licensed houses in the first decade of the 20th century. Its first recorded mention was in 1742 when the innholder, Thomas Heath, left a probate inventory valued at £18 10s. In 1819 the **Green Dragon** was given as being a change of address for a dyer, opposite. The inn was mentioned again in 1822 and in 1859 when the landlord was William Price. In 1888 William Poole was listed as licensed victualler and brewer. In 1895, or earlier, Mrs. Margaret Poole took over the business as owner and occupier and ran it as a free house. With a rateable value of £16 10s., the three-storey building comprised a parlour, tap room, kitchen, and

*The **Trotting Horse** in 2001.*

six bedrooms. Some time before 1911 it lost its licence and became a private residence.

Unmistakable is the pink-painted brick-faced private residence called Trotter House, at No. 102, which used to be an ancient inn known, amongst other names, as the **Trotting Horse**. There was a **Hunting Horse** listed in 1742 and in 1792 an **Old Running Horse**, both of which may have been earlier names. It may also have been the 17th-century inn called the **Harp**, which is included in the 1626 list..

The inn, which comprised a bar, parlour, kitchen and five bedrooms with stabling for two horses, came to be owned by the Ludlow Brewery, conveniently situated across the street. In 1868 the landlord was Richard Coleman followed by Charles James Grosvenor in 1888 who stayed there until about 1901. George Parnell was the landlord in 1926, but by 1937, soon after the Brewery was demolished, the **Trotting Horse** had closed its doors.

The **Nag's Head** at No. 126 was built in the 1840s on land that had lain vacant ever since the Civil War. It started its life first as a private house and was probably lived in for a time by a former French cavalry officer who settled in England after marrying one of the daughters of a land-owning family called Syer who hailed from Onibury.

A nag is a small riding horse or pony and early inn signs probably indicated that one could be had for hire from the inn. The inn was

The Nag's Head in 1960.

certainly a calling point for carriers from the local villages of Aston and Aston Munslow, but it had no stabling of its own. It was also the nearest pub to the railway station, which must have been good for trade. The premises consisted of several drinking areas with a bar, taproom, smoke-room and sitting room (and seven bedrooms above) and it seemed to be a place for heavy drinking. For instance in 1892, the landlord, possibly Machell Wilson who was certainly there in 1888, was fined the hefty sum of £4 12s., with 8s. costs, for supplying beer to drunken persons. Five years later a case for permitting gaming was dismissed, and in 1899 the next landlord, Arthur Ward, was charged with permitting drunkenness, but the case was again dismissed.

Arthur Ward was still there in 1901 when the owners were the Brent Brewery Company of Liverpool. It was probably Ward who, in that same year, advertised for sale brewing plant consisting of a 180-gallon steel furnace, a 60-gallon small furnace, and a large mash tun (200 gallons).

Thomas Edwards was landlord in 1926 when trade received another fillip with the building of a new livestock market adjacent to the railway station and right behind the inn, the market replacing the Smithfield in Lower Galdeford. George Oliver Jones was the landlord

in 1941. The pub was later taken over
by Mitchells & Butlers, part of the
Bass empire, but was sold in the
1980s as a free house. As such it was
unsuccessful and by 1989 the **Nag's
Head** had closed. Since then the
building has been used as a stationers
and printers and then residential with
the main front bar area run as a
chocolate shop and now 'Fancy
That', a toy shop. The original inn
sign bracket is still in position.

*The **Nag's Head** in 2001.*

Another inn that was owned by
the Ludlow Brewery was the **Star and
Garter** at No. 138, which had also
been called the **Star Vaults** and simply the **Star**. The star & garter is a
reference to the Most Noble Order of the Garter, the highest order of
knighthood in Britain, instituted by Edward III about 1348. The story
goes that the king picked up the garter accidentally dropped by the
Countess of Salisbury. Noticing looks from the spectators, the king put
the garter round his own knee, exclaiming 'Honi soit qui mal y pense'.
The star forms part of the Order's insignia.

The first mention of the **Star & Garter** is in 1822, when
it was listed as one of Ludlow's principal inns. Then in 1840 it was put
up for sale by auction:

> The entire household goods and furniture, china, glass and
> earthenware, together with all the brewing utensils, casks etc. of the
> late Mrs. Palmer (hogsheads, half hogsheads and smaller casks,
> coolers and mashing tubs, tunpails, pails and buckets).

The inn continued to function, however, and by 1859 the landlord
was Thomas Coston. William Powell Griffiths had taken over by 1888
when it was called **Star Vaults**; Henry Carter was the licensee in 1900.
The inn was a posting house with good stabling for 12 horses
(although the licensing return for 1901 noted that the stables
required whitewashing). Carriers operated to the villages of
Broadstone, Leintwardine, and Vernolds Common. According to the
Kelly's Directory for 1900 the inn provided 'excellent luncheons on

*An outing from the **Star** towards the end of the 19th century.*

market day, every other Monday' served in the dining room. Other accommodation included a bar and smoke room, kitchen and four bedrooms. The rateable value in 1901 was assessed at £44.

It was re-named the **Star Hotel** when the sign showed: 'Wines and Spirits, Fine Ales and Stout, good stabling, loose boxes'.

A picture taken some time between 1910 and 1919

*The **Star and Garter** in 1960.*

shows the landlord, Frederick William Curtis, with other members of the Ludlow Licensed Victuallers' Association, standing by a horse-drawn coach outside the **Star** in readiness for an outing. Like the **Nag's Head**, the inn benefited from the opening of the new cattle auction yards in the 1920s and whose own yard gave access to them.

*The conversion to flats has completely changed the façade of the **Star and Garter**.*

'Good accommodation' was advertised in 1941 when Frederick George Heath was in charge. But the inn closed in 1964 under the brewers ownership change that also resulted in the closure of the **Barley Mow**. In 1973 the premises entered a new lease of life. The main building was converted into three flats and three houses were built in the Star yard.

In 1626, recognisances to sell beer or ale were granted to over 100 Ludlow residents, but only 16 of these had inns known by their signs. One of these 16 was the **Talbot Inn** at Nos. 139 and 139a, but it was no longer present in the 1792 list of inns in Corve Street. The name derived from the 15th-century Talbot family, who used the hunting-dog (white with black spots) on their coat of arms. Today the

site is ocupied by 'New Image', hairdressers, and Garrard antiques. The former malthouse and kiln, which lie behind No. 139a, is where Leonard Davies operated as an estate agent, specialising in the licensed trade in 1941.

The 1626 list also included the **Rose & Crown** at No. 145, so it

*Once the **Talbot**.*

must have been of some importance. Perhaps it survived the Civil War clearance because the sign indicated loyalty to the monarch and to England. It was still listed as one of the larger Ludlow inns in 1672, but is not mentioned in a licensing list of 1792. Today an imposing two-storey brick house stands on the site.

In the 18th century there used to be an inn called the **Spread Eagle** at No. 148. The name originated from the Roman eagle, emblazoned on their battle standards, and was taken up by English noble families on their coats of arms after the Crusades. The inn is mentioned in a list of licensed premises for 1742, 1792, and 1822. In 1859 the landord is given as Benjamin Breakwell. The licence was dropped and in 1872 it became a 'cottage'. The last tenant of the **Spread Eagle** had been Anne Massey. The inn was later demolished to make way for a shopping development. In the early 1920s Sale and Higginson, ironmongers, were at No. 148, followed in later years by another ironmongers. Today the 'Silver Pear' displays its gift wares.

The earliest record of the **Holy Lamb** at No. 151 is in 1742 when William Ible, the innholder, left a probate inventory valued at £19 4s. 6d. In Christian art, the lamb represents Jesus Christ, an allusion to John's 'Behold the Lamb of God, which taketh away the sins of the world'. As a saintly emblem a lamb accompanies John the Baptist and others. By 1790 the inn has dropped the 'Holy' and had William Hand as innkeeper. The 'Holy' returned in 1822, but was dropped again in 1859 when John Evans was in charge, and in the 1870s the inn closed and the building was demolished. The site was then cleared to make way for new shops. Today, even the number 151 has disappeared.

CHAPTER ELEVEN

Tower Street & Galdeford

Ludlow's Galdeford Tower and Gate had quite another purpose than being part of the town's defensive wall. Built in the 13th century, the tower was used as the town goal and prisoners could lanquish there in great squalor for years before trial. By 1764 both Tower and Gate had fallen into disrepair and were demolished. Another grim stone building, described as a 'commodious edifice', was constructed on the same site to become the new gaol. It cost £422 and was designed by Shrewsbury architect Thomas Farnolls Pritchard.

The 13th and 14th centuries were particularly violent with many killings or murders committed in the town caused by drink exacerbated by a plethora of swords and knives. Thus, in the year 1271:

> Wyn Forester of Stanton Lacy stabbed Roger Lyde with his sword while they were returning from a Ludlow tavern; in the same year Thomas Gyllur knifed Elias Spark of Onibury at Robert Dul's tavern [probably at No. 37 Broad Street]; Richard Acton stabbed to death Richard Mideltone outside another Ludlow tavern; similarly Thomas Stoke killed his brother Roger.

An early system for apprehending suspected felons was to call out the hue and cry, armed neighbours who went in pursuit 'with horn and with voice'. This often led to summary lynching, but Shropshire juries in those days were surprisingly merciful—of 48 men accused of felonious killing in Ludlow in the middle part of Edward I's reign, only five were hanged, 16 were acquitted, while no fewer than 22 fled and either sought sanctuary in churches or were outlawed.

After Edward IV's charter of 1461 Ludlow had its own town court with the ability to pass capital sentences—a man, or woman, could be

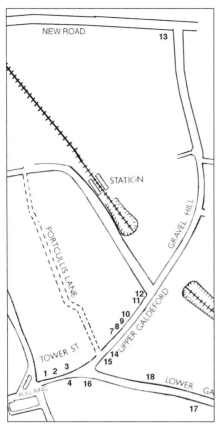

Tower Street and Galdeford.

hanged for such offences as 'picking purses'. The prisoner was taken from Galdeford Gaol to Gallow's Bank above Sheet Road, where the gibbet was visible from the town. (The word 'galdeford', spelt 'goalford' in the 19th century, indeed comes from the way or ford to the gallows). For less serious offences Ludlow provided a range of other punishments. In 1601 the town had a 'whipping master' under contract who would whip one person for 2d. or give a group discount and whip four people for 6d! Flogging was carried out at either the Market House whipping post or through the town behind a cart, as happened to Elizabeth Fisher in 1604. A label might be affixed to the prisoner's back with such words as 'a notorious cheat'.

The earliest reference to the pillory is in 1556 when 'a false accuser (was) burnt in both cheeks and put upon the pillory'. Then in 1576, Richard Hall was paid '12d. for nailing three men on the pillory', presumably by the ears. There was also a 'cage', which was frequently in need of repair, well into the 17th century.

156

In the 16th century wilful poisoning was regarded as one of the worst crimes imaginable with a punishment that was equally horrible. Ancient criminal records in Ludlow revealed: 'Also, there was a cooke boyled in Smithfield for poysoning' and 10 years later 'in 1541, a mayde boyled in Smithfield for poisoning three householders'. Boiling to death was the then statutory punishment for wilful poisoning.

A ducking or gumble stool was used in the Teme or the Corve for women such as Mary Derby accused of being a 'drunkard, swearer, curser and common scold' in 1600. A pillory was on permanent display at the Castle Square end of Mill Street, while the stocks were either outside the workhouse in Old Street or at the Market House. The law made minimal allowance for the age of the accused—at that time in the eyes of the law children over the age of eight were adults.

It was nationally enacted in 1605, and again in 1623, that upon conviction, the punishment for drunkards should be a fine of 5s. and 6 hours in the stocks. Tippling on Sunday, during the hours of divine service, was punished by a spell in the stocks till quite a late period— well into the 19th century.

Often men were charged with being drunk in charge of a horse and trap. The horse would be put up for the night at the inn while the defendant would walk or be driven home. In July 1886 Joseph Gough was sentenced by Ludlow magistrates to six weeks' hard labour for being drunk in charge of a donkey and cart. Perhaps Gough was a persistent offender to warrant such a harsh sentence!

At the turn of the 20th century crime was still commonplace and much drinking continued to take place in Ludlow alehouses. The Town Crier would go around the town to make a proclamation warning against thieves.

To become drunk and abusive near the police station and on Christmas Eve is perhaps a trifle foolhardy, but this is what George Wilkes, a labourer, contrived to do. He was charged with being drunk and disorderly on 24 December 1910, P.C. Mills stating that he saw the defendant at 10.45 p.m. in Tower Street, shouting and making use of bad language. Wilkes was dressed up as a woman, and had his face blacked. He had a large crowd round him, and his conduct was very bad. P.C. Mills had to threaten to lock him up before he would go away. The defendant, who pleaded guilty, was fined 5s. including costs, or 7 days' imprisonment.

The Town Gaol subsequently became the police station, and was demolished in the 1950s. The site and adjoining superintendent's house is now part of Dillons store.

Named after the Tower, and pedestrianised since 1989, Tower Street is a short stretch of road leading eastwards from the town centre. The road narrows where the Gate once stood and then branches out to become Upper and Lower Galdeford (or Gaolford as it is pronounced locally due to the name's origins).

In addition to the **Pheasant**, which stood on the corner with Old Street (and is described in chapter 9), Tower Street also supported another four inns. On the north side at No. 7 was the **Black Boy**, which may have been the **Buck's Head** (normally a reference to the male deer) mentioned in 1773 and again in 1790 when the landlord was Thomas Morris. Alternatively it may have been the **Blue Lion** (either an association with Queen Anne, wife of James I and mother of Charles I, or just because the inn's front door was painted blue).

The inn had definitely become the **Black Boy** by 1820 when a small poster appeared stating: 'James George, drainer, seeking draining work, said letters could be sent to him at Mr. Bright's Black Boy Inn, Ludlow'. In the 17th and 18th centuries the sign referred to the personal servant of a rich person, at a time when negro page-boys were extremely fashionable. In 1859 the landlord was given as Thomas Jenkins and in 1888 it was William Henry Medlicott, described as licensed victualler and 'commission agent'. In 1894 the landlord was fined £3 with costs of 14s. 6d. for permitting drunkenness on the premises. Henry Fawkes was the landlord in 1900, but a year later it was Harold Stanley, of Birmingham, with the inn then owned by Ind Coope & Co. That same year, when a licensing inspection was carried out, the **Black Boy**, which had held a full licence since about 1840, had a rateable value of £15 10s. The inn comprised a bar, kitchen, parlour, clubroom and three bedrooms. There was no stabling.

Although the police station was only two doors away, at No. 9, the police protested that they could not keep a proper eye on the inn as people could hide in alleyways. Shortly afterwards the **Black Boy** closed and became a fishmongers. Eventually, this and the adjoining sweet shop at No.8 were demolished to make way for the Shrewsbury Co-operative Society. For a while the building was occupied by a government department, but it is now derelict.

The **Crown and Horses** may have existed at Nos. 10-11. At any rate the landlord, John Prodgers, a blacksmith by trade, is recorded as having moved to the **Feathers** in 1756. There is no reference to the name in a list of inns of 1792, but the **Royal Oak** certainly did exist at No. 13. After the **Red Lion**, the name became the second most popular inn sign in the country. It originated from the celebration of Charles II's birthday on 29 May as Royal Oak thanksgiving day. This was a reference to his ecape from Roundhead soldiers after hiding from noon to dusk in the Boscobel Oak, at Shifnal near Telford, in 1651. The inn is first mentioned in 1743 and again in 1790 when the landlord was Thomas Amiss. In 1859 the landlord was Thomas Pearce and in 1888 Lousia Patrick was described as both licensed victualler and brewer. Then, apparently in a drive to reduce the number of pubs in Ludlow, its licence was revoked and the building was allowed to fall into decay.

The site was bought cheaply and rebuilt as the Royal Oak Café and Temperance Hotel. In 1900, with Mrs. E.A. Adams as manageress, it was open 'for cyclists, commercials, etc with beds, dinners, teas, refreshment'. Richard Alfred Fletcher was the proprietor in 1926, and in 1941, when it was described as the Royal Oak Café and Temperance Hall, it was owned by Thomas Dobson. By the 1950s it had closed and for a while a shop was opened on the ground floor. Eventually the building was demolished and the site is now part of Somerfield Stores.

On the south side of Tower Street, opposite the Tower goal, once stood the **Talbot**, the third inn in Ludlow with the same name (see Broad Street and Corve Street). The inn, probably built in about 1760, is included in a list of licensed houses of 1822. The following year, a poster appeared:

> To be let, and entered upon at Lady Day next The **Talbot Inn** together with the house occupied by Mr. Perry, a Blacksmith's Shop, Stables, Brewhouse and Premises, now in the occupation of Mr. Loveridge, situate in Tower Street. These premises have been used as an inn for more than 60 years, and the situation being near the Cattle, Sheep and Pig Markets, render it very desirable.

Auctions were often held at the inn, but the one conducted in 1825 was rather special. A poster proclaimed:

To inn-keepers and others, Ludlow, stock-in-trade, household furniture, casks, brewing utensils etc. to be sold by auction by Mr. Bach on Thursday, 9 June 1825 on the premises of the Talbot Inn. All the stock in trade, genuine household furniture and other effects late the property of Mr. Edward Rea, malster and inn keeper. Consisting of 4-post, tent and other bedsteads, with cotton and other furniture, prime feather, and flock beds, with bedside carpets, swing glasses, night tables and basin stands, an excellent assortment of bed and table linen, blankets, quilts and counter-panes; a variety of china, glass and earthenware, dining and breakfast tables, bureas, parlour, bedroom and kitchen chairs, excellent 8-day clock in oak case, an iron furnace, and a general assortment of kitchen requisites. Also, the stock of spirits, strong beer, ale, cider, casks of all descriptions in excellent preservation, brewing utensils and various other effects.

The above Inn and premises will be let to a respectable tenant at a moderate rent, and may be entered upon immediately. The dwelling house, with the stable, buildings, yard and premises are very spacious, in good repair, capable of carrying on an extensive business, have been long established and are now well accustomed, the situation thereof is desirable, and a deserving tenant will meet every encouragement.

A few years later the **Talbot**'s stable and yard gave way to a house, which stood there in 1833. A meeting of the Ludlow Conservatives was held at the inn in 1840. In 1859 the landlord was Joseph Weaver, but the inn did not appear in a list of licensed houses for 1888. Part of the Ludlow Club, with an address given as 12a Tower Street, may now stand on the site of the old **Talbot**.

In 1760 a **Dog** near Galdeford Gate and a **Dog** without Galdeford Gate were listed; but in a list of inns for 1792 there is no mention of any kind of **Dog** in Galdeford.

Continuing along to Upper Galdeford on the north side at No. 3 used to be the **Bell**, the first of a block of four inns situated side by side. It was first recorded in 1744 and mentioned again in 1792. A reminder of the harshness of those days and how easy it was to end up in prison is vividly brought home in a poster dated March 1821 concerning William Fosbrooke, the former landlord of the **Bell**. Entitled 'Pray

Remember the Poor Debtor' and addressed 'to the Charitable, and Humane disposed persons of the town of Ludlow and its environs', the poster described the landlord's tale of woe.

The **Bell** was sold for £360 in 1830 but the fate of the unfortunate Mr. Fosbrooke is not known. In 1859 the inn was run by Benjamin

TO THE
Charitable, and Humane
DISPOSED PERSONS OF THE TOWN OF
LUDLOW,
AND ITS ENVIRONS.

UNDER the following peculiar circumstances, WILLIAM FOSBROOKE, late of the *Bell-Inn*, in *Goalford*, but now a Debtor in his Majesty's Jail for the Town of LUDLOW, being afflicted with a very long and painful Illness, which confined him to his Bed for two Years, and having lost the use of his Limbs, (the expences naturally attendant upon these calamities) has reduced him to the most deplorable condition, and to add to his afflictions, his Landlord who had been promised by responsible persons that his full Rent should be paid, in case his Goods would produce that amount, consented to abide the event of a Sale, *afterwards forfeited his word by levying a Distress;* To increase the Poor Man's misery, after his Goods were Sold to the last penny's-worth, a Creditor, (although he had no possible chance of receiving any Money,) Arrested his poor helpless Body, when confined to his Bed, and from thence conveyed to Prison on a Man's Back, where he now lies destitute of every support, *but the common Jail allowance.*---- A Subscription is therefore proposed to be set on foot, not to encourage the dishonest Debtor, but to countenance and give nourishment to this honest and unfortunate Man, and alleviate as much as possible the afflictions under which he now lies; It is respectfully recommended to all CHARITABLE and HUMANE Persons, to consider his very distressed situation, and Subscribe towards his relief, he having always supported an honest Character through life.

N. B. It is proposed that the Subscription shall be under the direction of a Committee, who will distribute it to Mrs. FOSBROOKE, as they think proper, and the said Committee will afterwards publish the names of the Subscribers, and also render an Account of the disbursement, which may be seen at the Printing-Office, where Subscriptions will be thankfully received. March 27th 1821.

Ludlow, Printed at the Office of T. Griffiths in the Bull-Ring.

The plea for William Fosbrooke.

Miller and in 1888 by William Froggatt, described as licensed victualler and brewer. In 1901 the inn was owned by Kezia Froggatt, presumably William's widow, who had been running the inn for the past five years. According to a licensing return of the same year, the inn consisted of a bar, smoke room, kitchen and seven bedrooms with stables for three horses. It had possessed a full licence since about 1800 and its rateable value was £16 10s. Shortly afterwards the inn lost its licence as part of the authorities efforts to reduce the number of pubs in Ludlow, and the building became a family run grocery shop for more than 50 years. Eventually it was demolished and, like its neighbour, the **Royal Oak**, the site is now part of Somerfield Store.

Next door at No. 5 was the **Three Horse Shoes** or just the **Horseshoes**, as it was called in 1790 when Edward Jones was the innkeeper. The name referred to the Worshipful Company of Farriers, although a single horseshoe was usually associated with a reputation for being lucky. Samuel T. Lugg was mine host in 1859 and George Butcher was licensed victualler and brewer in 1888. In 1893, a case brought against the landlord for supplying whisky to a drunken person was dismissed, but another case in 1897, for permitting drunkenness, brought

*The **Three Horseshoes** in 1960.*

a fine of 50s. with 30s. costs.

William Butcher was the owner, with James Corbett as occupier, when a licensing inspection was carried out in 1901. This showed that the inn, which had a rateable value of £39, comprised a bar, parlour, kitchen and five bedrooms. There was stabling for 20 horses. Corbett was also described as a hay and straw dealer and the inn was the base for carriers to Bitterley, Burwarton, and Stoke St. Milborough. Behind the **Three Horseshoes** was the

Lion Mineral Water Works, operated by F.W. Beeston, manufacturers of every kind of mineral waters and bottler of Burton Ales and Dublin Stout.

In 1926 the landlord was George Arthur Fuller, who was still there in 1941. His widow, Mrs. Sally Fuller, continued to run the place until 1967 when the **Three Horshoes** closed its doors for the last time. Sally had a reputation for clean floors, and according to Harry Baker, 'one room had large stone flags so spotless it was said you could eat off them, and the other was of wood, scrubbed and sanded every day so that the planks were snowy white'. The inn was bought by the Borough Council, demolished and a road constructed across the site leading to the Somerfield and Upper Galdeford car parks.

The third pub in the terrace was the **Dolphin** at No. 7. It is first mentioned in 1743 and again in 1792. In January 1821 a poster appeared:

Lost—a bundle of leather, 33lb. weight. Whoever has found same, and will return it to Mr. Cantrill, Dolphin Inn, Ludlow or to Mr. John Dolphin, Hopton Bank, shall receive a half guinea reward.

In 1859 the landlord was William Price and in 1888 it was William Poulter. The inn closed soon afterwards and became two shops, but the name lingered on with the Dolphin Café at No. 7, which was also the Ludlow terminus for the Midland Red bus parcels service. The building was eventually demolished to make way for a block of flats.

The last in the row of four and the last to close was the **Portcullis**, at No. 13, which stood on an ancient site but which took up the name after the **Blue Boar** forsook it in 1739. The name was a popular heraldic device and was associated with both Henry VII and Henry VIII. In this case it was an apposite choice with the inn being on the corner of Portcullis Lane and close to Galdeford Gate, which originally had a portcullis. The first record of the **Portcullis**, when it was a half-timbered thatched building, was in 1756. It was mentioned again in 1790, when the innkeeper was Joseph Price.

A poster of 1881 declared:

Portcullis Inn, Goalford—sale of Household Furniture, Brewery Utensils, Casks, Beer Engine, Trams, Copper furnace, the property of Mrs. Bourne.

Millward & Norton have received instructions to sell by auction, 21st March, 1881.—Bar Parlour, Brewhouse—brewery equipment.

The three-pull beer engine, with lead piping, was sold to Mr. W. Pugh for £1 15s. He also bought other items, including spittoons, for 2s.

The new landlord, at any rate by 1888, was Charles Miller, who was also a blacksmith. Extensive stabling at the rear enabled the inn to function as one of the town's leading cart carriers with, in 1885, eight departures a week to Brown Clee Hill, Clee Hill, and Hopton's Bank. Soon after the inn was bought by Ind Coope & Co., who rebuilt it as a large red-brick building offering bar, parlour, smokeroom, kitchen, clubroom and six bedrooms. Stabling was for 25 horses. Its rateable value was assessed at £29 15s. in 1901, when the landlord was Robert Gamble, who had been there for five years. Gamble also described himself as a 'hay and straw salesman and saddle and harness maker'.

Mrs. Bertha Abbott was landlady in 1926, and in 1941 it was Bertie Greenhill, who had been the last licensee of the **Vaults** in the Bull Ring. In the early 1950s, when road accidents were much rarer than they are now, he was knocked down and killed by a car while crossing Corve Street to go to the Post Office. It was at about this time, in 1951, that fire broke out in a back bedroom of the inn one lunch-time. The patrons went on drinking, it was reported, while firemen put out the fire. Damage was extensive—a 12ft. by 11ft. hole in the front roof, while part of the back roof caved in. One of the last landlords was Mr. D.T.E. Lloyd, who became Mayor of Ludlow in 1988 and 1989. The inn closed soon after when it became a doctor's surgery, was later demolished and the site is now absorbed into a residential estate.

Nearby was another inn called the **Vine**, on a pathway that led to the Labour Club. It may previously have been the **Bricklayers Arms**, mentioned in 1748. Neither name was recorded in 1790.

There was at least one malthouse in the street. A poster of 1821 announced: 'To be let and entered upon at Michalmas next a Dwelling House situate in Upper Goalford with an excellent Malthouse adjoining, capable of Wetting and Drying off 70 bushels of barley'.

Further along Upper Galdeford, at the junction with Gravel Hill where Station Road commences, used to be the **Greyhound**. When it was first recorded in 1841, with William Thompson as victualler, it lay a short distance beyond the old borough boundary in an area that was then being developed. In 1859, his widow, Sarah was the innkeeper, but by 1888 the licensed victualler was John Rollings, who was also described as being a 'blacksmith'. In 1889 the landlord was fined 1s. with 6s. costs for supplying drink during prohibited hours. In a return of licensed houses of 1896 in the Petty Sessional Divison of Lower Munslow, the inn was owned by Henry Lloyd, of Ludlow, and occupied by William Watts, who was the manager. The inn, which had a rateable value of £19 and had held a full licence since 1840, consisted of a kitchen, two parlours, bar and four

*The **Greyhound Inn** is remembered by the road sign on a modern house.*

bedrooms with stabling for four horses. William Watts was still there in 1900, but by 1926 the landlord was Charles Morris.

The **Greyhound** (the heraldic reference of this name is to the dukes of Newcastle, owners of land in many parts of the country) closed in 1937 when its then owner sold the full licence to the Bridge cider house at Dorrington. It was used as a private house until it was demolished in the early 1980s. The name lingers on as there are Greyhound road names on the houses on both sides of Station Road.

Further along, where Gravel Hill joins New Road, is the **Raven** (the bird was sacred to the Druids, and it is said that in the late 17th century use of the sign indicated Jacobite sympathies on the part of the innkeeper). The inn was built to cater for the developing East Hamlet area and soon became a focus for the new suburbs which before long had a few shops and a school. In a survey of 1841 James Harding was listed as 'victualler' at the inn. With market towns being places of passage, people moved around for work, and it is recorded that in 1861 five clogmakers from Lancashire stayed at the **Raven**. In 1888 the licensed victualler was George Griffiths. In the

*The **Raven** in 2002.*

1896 return of licensed houses the **Raven**, which had a rateable value of £24, was described as having a kitchen, bar, parlour, club room and four bedrooms. There was stabling for 10 horses. A free house, it was owned by Henry Lloyd and occupied by Henry Rogers, who ran the business himself. In 1900, according to *Kelly's Directory*, Henry Rogers was also landlord of the **Wheatsheaf** in Lower Broad Street. The inn is now owned by Enterprise Inns who bought it from Bass and it is still very much a 'community pub'.

On the other side of New Road, near the junction with New Street, was a beerhouse appropriately called the **New Inn**, but its exact location is uncertain. It was opened in about 1850 to help cater for the needs of the developing East Hamlet area and in 1900 it was run by Mrs. Susan Crowther. Shortly afterwards, however, it closed down.

On the south side of the road going back into town, near the junction with Lower Galdeford, was an inn originally called the **Fox** (a name which allowed sign-writers full reign for their comic sense of design), which had been operating a full licence since about 1600. A **Fox** is mentioned in 1742 and in 1745 there is both an **Old Fox** and a **New Fox**. In 1749 there is a **Lower Fox** and in 1753 an **Upper Fox**, but by 1792 there was apparently no **Fox** in Galdeford at all. However, the name reappeared in 1822, and in 1859 the licensed victualler was given as John Thomas.

By the 1870s the inn had been renamed the **Birmingham Arms** (probably in honour of the Midlands city which was developing quickly in the mid-19th century) and in 1888 it was run by Thomas Lewis, who was also described as a malster and a brewer. In 1899 the landlord was fined 20s. for selling drink to a drunken person. By 1901 it was owned by Ind Coope & Co. with John Bytheway as licensed victualler. With a rateable value of £19, it consisted of a bar, smoke-room, kitchen and five bedrooms. Some time before 1910, the **Birmingham Arms** went out of existence and the site was redeveloped. The *Ludlow Advertiser* offices stood there from 1914, but these too moved, and today the site is occupied by Paul George, Butchers and Gelli's Pizza Restaurant.

A few doors along was another **New Inn**, (many New Inns came into being in the 16th century as a result of Elizabeth I's complaints about the lack of suitable places for travellers to stay). The first listing of this **New Inn** was in 1770 but it was no longer mentioned by 1792. However, it was identified on the present site in the 1850s when Gravel Hill and Sandpits began to expand, and it belonged to the Perry family for more than 60 years. By 1888 the licensed victualler was William Perry, who was the owner and brewed his own beer. In 1900 William Perry described himself also as 'a hay salesman' and the **New Inn** operated as a calling point for cart carriers from such villages as Clee St. Margaret, Clee Hill, Hope Bagot, Hopton's Bank, Knowbury, and Stoke St. Milborough. This is not surprising because a licensing return of 1901 shows there was stabling for eight horses. The pub itself was quite small consisting of a kitchen, parlour, back kitchen and three bedrooms. It had a rateable value of £18 and trade was described as 'agricultural, and in town'.

Mr. Perry was a keen angler, and a photograph taken in 1908 shows the landlord with 20 lbs. of roach and dace he caught in two hours. Another photo, taken in about 1910, shows a group of mounted soldiers of the South Shropshire Yeomanry outside the **New Inn**, with its sign advertising that wines and spirits and 'Pure Home Brewed Ales' were sold. Yet another old photo shows the **New Inn**, now covered in ivy, after the Great War with a gathering of young

*Mr. Perry, landlord of the **New Inn**, with the fish he caught in two hours.*

motorcyclists outside. The inn was the headquarters of Ludlow Town Football Club and Ludlow Angling Society. By 1926 it was still the headquarters of these two organisations and William Joseph Perry had become a member of the Severn Board of Conservators. Then, in the mid-1930s, William James Perry. presumably the son, came to a macabre end. While brewing one day, he was overcome by fumes and fell head first into an upright barrel and was drowned. The coroner recorded a verdict of 'Accidental death'. According to Harry Baker's father, a somewhat snide remark going round the town at that time was that even if

*Soldiers of the South Shropshire Yeomanry outside the **New Inn** c.1910.*

it had been suicide, it was while temporarily insane, 'because nobody in his right mind would touch Bill Perry's beer'!

The licence was abandoned in 1970 and the building was bought as a private residence. Some time later it reverted to commercial use becoming a veterinary surgery, an office for a security firm and then, about 1999, the Ludlow Fish Bar and Restaurant.

*The Ludlow Fish Bar and Restaurant was previously the **New Inn**.*

At the town end of Lower Galdeford, where it joins Upper Galdeford and Tower Street, is the **Queen's Head**, which survives today. Built on vacant land in about 1841 and named after Queen Victoria, it boasted a large yard and extensive stabling to cater for the expanding suburbs. In 1888 the licensed victualler was Charles Guest, who was also a farmer and timber merchant. The 1901 licensing return showed that it could stable as many as 20 horses. The inn itself, which had a rateable value of £30, consisted of a bar, kitchen, billiard room,

*Forceful advertising on the **Queen's Head** in the early 20th century.*

169

*Quoits was a serious activity at the **Queen's Head**, judging by the expressions on the faces of the team members.*

*The **Queen's** is now a pub and cafe bar.*

and four bedrooms. The owner and occupier was George Griffiths who had been there for at least five years. He also described himself as a 'hay and straw dealer'. Later the yard was used as the base for a private bus service going to Knowbury and Clee Hill. In 1926 the landlord was Harry Johns and in 1941 it was the rather exotic sounding Chas. G. Le Comte. Today, the inn is called simply the

Queen's and operates as a coffee bar as well as a pub.

Further down the road, at No. 67, was the **Smithfield**, which was built in the early 1860s at the same time as the site of the old Austin Friary was being developed as Ludlow's new cattle market. The name means smooth field and was originally a place where horses were sold, but later came to be associated with cattle. While Smithfield, the market, closed down in 1900, when a new one was built nearer the railway, **Smithfield**, the pub, remained trading for another 80 years.

*The **Smithfield** is now a private house.*

It started as a beerhouse, but James Conley, who bought the place, developed it into a full licence by 1867, when he was described as owner/occupier. The **Smithfield** remained in the Conley family for more than 50 years. In 1900 Mrs. Sarah Conley was the landlady, but in the licensing return of 1901, the owner/occupier was given as Thomas James Conley, presumably her son. The inn consisted of a bar, parlour, tap room and three bedrooms. The brewing of home-made beer was a feature but, according to the return, the brewhouse 'required whitewashing'.

In about 1920 the **Smithfield** was run by a Mr. Morris, who was also a railway ganger, and his wife. Their son, Thomas, who still enjoys a pint of beer in one of the Ludlow pubs at the age of 81, said he was born there, one of six children. 'I remember beer, when it was real beer, costing 4¹/₂d. a pint. Every week in the 1920s', he recalled, 'about 150 men working on the Birmingham Water Works went to the **Smithfield** to get paid. They built a pipe to take water from Elan in Wales to Birmingham. Hundreds of thirsty men worked as navvies on the water works and also on the railways'. William Nutt was the landlord in 1926 and Arthur Etheridge in 1941, the inn surviving until after 1983, but is now a private residence—a pink-painted brick, three-storey building.

On the opposite side of the road, at No. 13, was the **Half Moon**, identified today by two porch columns jutting out onto the pavement. The inn, originally called the **Mitre**, dates back to the early 17th century, but, like many other properties in Lower Galdeford, was indiscriminately burnt down during the Civil War. The present premises date back to about 1700 when they were let at an annual rent of 6s. 8d. The name was changed to the **Half Moon** in 1770 and is mentioned in the 1790 list of inns, when the landlord was William Pugh. It appears that 'old Mr Pugh' died in January 1827 and that another Mr. Pugh, presumably his son, died earlier, in August 1826. John Davis was in charge in 1859.

The *Ludlow Advertiser* of 6 December 1885 reported:

A Drunken Tailor

John Grace, tailor, drunk and disorderly in street. Landlord of the Half Moon Inn asked P.C. to turn defendant out of the yard. Pushed him into street and told him to go home. He was fined 10s., including costs, or seven days hard labour.

In 1888 the owner and occupier was Alexander Whitbread, who was also described as a bricklayer and builder. In the 1901 licensing return, the **Half Moon** had a rateable value of £29 and comprised a bar, kitchen, smokeroom, and five bedrooms. There was stabling for eight

horses. The owner/occupier was still Mr. Whitbread and he remained there throughout the First World War, following which his son, Herbert, was caretaker/landlord until its closure at the end of the 1920s. The family name lives on in nearby Whitbread Road, in memory of one of Herbert's sons, Laurie, a Spitfire pilot, who was killed in 1940 during the Battle of Britain.

*The **Half Moon** in 2002.*

CHAPTER TWELVE

The Neighbouring Villages

Whitcliffe Common overlooks the town from the south-west. Stone used to be quarried there which went into building much of old Ludlow, livestock was grazed, and hay and firewood gathered. Overlooking the Teme and town, it became a fashionable promenade in the 18th century, and in the mid-19th century a riverside walk was laid out.

Whitcliffe was often the setting for some of the old customs observed in Ludlow with such 'peculiar vitality', as someone once remarked. For instance, up to 1840, a Maypole was 'reared' regularly by New Bridge at the foot of Whitcliffe when open-air dances were held. Bonfire Day was another old custom when the procession marched through the town to Whitcliffe Hill, the appointed site of the bonfire. Sometimes the procession included as many as five effigies accompanied by bearers of lighted Chinese lanterns. Headed by a drum-and-fife band, the crowd marched to Whitcliffe, where the effigies were burnt, amidst fireworks and the shouts of the bystanders. Squibs and fireballs were freely kicked and flung about in all directions.

No doubt some of the revellers sought liquid refreshment at the conveniently situated **Ludlow Arms**, an old established inn on Whitcliffe Road. The inn was a 17th-century timber-framed building which was noted for its fine bowling green, reputedly 18th century in origin, and for a fives court of similar date. Over the years the inn bore the names of **Whitcliffe** and **Bowling Green** and was included in Nicolas Pevsner's notes on Ludlow in his guide book to Shropshire.

Local gentry used the bowling green and fives court, which must have been impressive with a large brick wall some 35ft. high by 30ft.

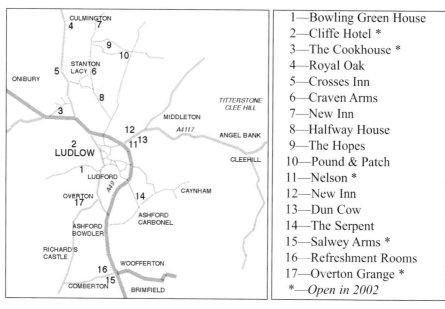

	1—Bowling Green House
	2—Cliffe Hotel *
	3—The Cookhouse *
	4—Royal Oak
	5—Crosses Inn
	6—Craven Arms
	7—New Inn
	8—Halfway House
	9—The Hopes
	10—Pound & Patch
	11—Nelson *
	12—New Inn
	13—Dun Cow
	14—The Serpent
	15—Salwey Arms *
	16—Refreshment Rooms
	17—Overton Grange *
	*—*Open in 2002*

The Surrounding Area.

broad and white lines rising 8ft. up the wall. Sometimes matches were staged between the gentlemen of Shropshire and those of neighbouring counties. There was even a fives ball maker living on Whitcliffe.

In a return of licensed houses for 1896, the **Ludlow Arms** was owned by Lord Windsor, of Oakly Park, and occupied by Henry Crane, who managed the freehouse property. This comprised a kitchen, bar, billiard room and three bedrooms with stabling for four horses. It held

*The **Ludlow Arms** from the bowling green.*

a full licence dating back to 1830 and the rateable value was £14 a year. The inn was in the Crane family for a number of years; in 1885 the licensee was Mrs. Catherine Crane, while in 1913 it was Mrs. Harry Crane.

The bowling green was well used in the 1920s and 1930s, when the inn

*The **Ludlow Arms** is now a private house.*

was popular with visitors from the Midlands. In 1968 it ceased trading as an inn, but carried on as a private hotel. In 1984 an advert appeared: 'Bowling Green House, Whitcliffe - the Tudor house is extremely comfortable with a log fire in the lounge and the bedrooms are both attractive and peaceful. Licensed à la carte restaurant. Under the personal supervision of Mary and Tony Gallop'. It must have been rather unsuccessful, for it eventually became a private house.

The Bowling Green on Whitcliff about 1910.

175

*The route to the **Cliffe Hotel** provides splendid views of Ludlow Castle.*

Leaving Whitcliffe Common towards Bromfield, one comes to Halton Lane and the **Cliffe Hotel** at Dinham. Originally a 19th-century gentleman's house, it was owned and occupied by Humphrey Salwey, solicitor, a relative of the family who were squires of Richard's Castle since the 17th century. Other gentry resided there until in 1941 it was turned into a boarding house and in 1971 it became a hotel. Tucked

*The original **Clive Arms**.*

*Bromfield Farm—the **Cookhouse** in 2001.*

away from the town, the **Cliffe** has a restaurant, bar and nine *en-suite* bedrooms.

To get to Bromfield, by car, it is necessary to go back into Ludlow and take the A49 towards Craven Arms, a busy road which cuts right through the village. On the west side is Oakly Park, home of the Windsor-Clives, descendants of Clive of India, and now the earls of Plymouth; on the east side is the **Cookhouse** at the **Clive Arms**, owned by the estate. The original old coaching inn, with stables for at least eight horses, was next door at **Clive House**. For years it had catered for the needs of villager and traveller alike, but, so the story goes, a brawl broke out one night in the 1860s and it was closed by the estate. However, an alternative story relates that it was forced to close at the turn of the 20th century in rather amusing circumstances. One of the Windsor-Clives, a maiden lady, was driven one day into Ludlow by coach. The coach driver imbibed a little too freely and, on the return journey, he fell asleep. Instead of going to Oakly Park, the horse drew up outside the **Clive Arms**. Outraged, the lady demanded the closure of the inn forthwith.

At any rate it was not until 1977 that the estate decided to re-open the **Clive Arms**, not at Clive House, but next door at Bromfield Farm, a large 18th-century farmhouse built of stone with a brick fascia added later. At first it continued to operate as a village pub, but about four or five years ago new tenants from London took over and changed its decor and name to the **Cookhouse**. There is now a Chelsea style restaurant and coffee bar, with a bar converted from an outbuilding. The latter boasts a stepped fire-place with bread oven and Clive's coat of arms, with the motto *Audacter et Sincere* (boldly and sincerely). The coat of arms came from St. Fagan's castle, near Cardiff, which used to be owned by the earl of Plymouth, who did not move to Oakly Park until after the Second World War. It originally hung outside, but when it began to deteriorate from the weather it was brought indoors.

To reach Culmington, take the B4365 across Ludlow golf course, or Old Field, where in the early part of the 19th century buck hunts were watched by large crowds. This was part of Ludlow's annual October celebrations. These commenced with a Bailiffs' Feast followed by the hunt and a ball given by the bailiffs in the evening, which signalled the start of the Ludlow Assemblies held fortnightly through the winter. Annual horse races were held there from 1725 and the space was also utilised for election

*The rather battered Clive coat of arms in the **Cookhouse**.*

177

*The **Royal Oak** in 2001.*

campaigns such as in 1832 when a cavalcade 'more than a mile in length' met at the Old Field.

Situated on the main road and servicing the village was the **Royal Oak** inn, which closed down some 12 years ago and is now a private house. According to the return of licensed houses of 1896, the inn consisted of a tap room, bar parlour, kitchen, sitting room and five bedrooms. There was stabling for two horses. The owner and occupier was Thomas Lawley, who managed the inn as a freehouse, and had been there for the past five years. The full licence had been granted in 1830. Lawley was still there in 1901, when the pub's rateable value was put at £20; John William Holt was landlord in 1913 and Douglas Robertson from 1922 to 1941. The last landlord was Roger Dunn, who ran the inn for about four years before selling it. He built a house on the site of the old stables, where he presently lives, and two homes have been built on the paddock. The workshop by Seifton Brook which runs past the property used to be the brewery and bakehouse. While the games room at the back with cellar and toilets has been demolished, a lot of original internal features have been retained such as the off-licence sales window just off the lounge, which used to be the bar, the staircase and black and red floor tiles. Wem Ales used to be sold there and over the front porch one can just make out '... for you ...', possibly 'Thanks for your custom'.

Travelling back towards Ludlow a turning to Stanton Lacy is reached—a parish which, before its boundaries shrunk in 1879, boasted numerous pubs and cider houses, but today there is no pub. The Craven family lived in the Manor for two centuries and owned large parts of the village, but in 1862 the earls of Craven sold their interests, some of which went to the Clive family of Oakly Park.

Before arriving at Stanton Lacy, there is a double dwelling on the west side where the **Crosses Inn** used to stand. An old market place, built in 1863, was situated on the other side of the road. The inn closed between 1851 and 1861, possibly because of the departure of the Craven family, and the change in village ownership.

*The **Crosses Inn** in 2001.*

Reaching a T-junction in the village the house opposite—the Old Post Office—was once the village pub, the **Craven Arms**. It was last recorded as an inn in 1861, the year before the Cravens left Stanton Lacy, and closed shortly after. In the 1841 census, Henry Edwards was listed as victualler of the inn. It later became a shop, then the post office and is now a private dwelling. The property was thatched until

*Once the **Craven Arms**, and latterly the Post Office.*

the 1950s, when it was given a shingle roof.

Heading towards Lower Hayton one comes to Woodside, a private house, but formerly the **New Inn**, the last pub in the parish to close. It was built in 1820, just beyond the boundary marking the end of the earl of Plymouth's estate, to cater for the increase in travellers along the 'toll road' to Ludlow, which had been improved with the coming of the railways. The original building consisted of two kitchens, a parlour, and five bedrooms and there were six fireplaces. An archway led to a cobbled yard with stables, and access to an off-sales with a cellar behind.

Charles Downs was landlord in 1881 and it appears he allowed under age drinking for in 1882 he was fined 20s. with 12s. 6d. costs for supplying liquors to children under 16 years of age. He was fined again in 1897, this time 10s. 6d. with 17s. costs, for selling adulterated gin.

Mrs. Ada Nott was in charge in 1922, while John Nott was landlord in 1923 and 1926.

The stables were used by the local football team as changing rooms with after-match baths taken in two zinc baths, while a dentist and a barber carried out their trade there. Games like pitch and toss and crown and anchor were played in the yard. In the mid-1950s the inn was modernised and the archway and stables demolished; a piece of land was purchased by the brewery to build a car park and toilet block, but the pub closed in 1957.

*In the **New Inn** beer garden in the 1920s where Ernest Edwards and Thomas Smout are being served by mine host, Mrs. Smith..*

Travelling back along the Peaton to Ludlow road one would have come upon the **Halfway House**, which closed around 1830 and was later demolished. As the name indicates, it was a convenient stopping place for travellers and one of a chain of public houses along the drovers' roads. It probably only served cider.

On the way towards Upper Hayton is Hopes Farm House, an old house built in stone with an extension in brick. It was once the **Hopes**, a public house and farm, which closed during the 1850s. The

*The **New Inn**, refurbished as a house, in 2001.*

survey of 1841 referred to it as a beerhouse, with Samuel Weaver as beerhouse keeper. The 1861 survey makes no mention of the **Hopes**.

The road continues up to the old Bullring, a busy market place 300 years ago with no fewer than five roads leading to it; now there are only three. The old drovers' road, Wrens Nest Lane, leads past an old

*The **Hopes** is now a farmhouse.*

drovers' spring on the west side and then reaches an old watering site. On the other side is the overgrown Titterhill Lane which ran down to the **Pound and Patch**, an old cider house, which closed about 1820. Cider houses were often situated along drovers' roads and had pounds in which the animals were enclosed at night. The building was then used as a private dwelling until the early 1900s, became derelict and its remains were demolished in the mid-1960s.

Returning to the A49 that by-passes Ludlow and heading south,

The inn sign — a modern impression of Admiral Lord Nelson!

the A4117 to Kidderminster is soon met at Rocks Green, where the 300-year-old **Nelson Inn** stands. It was originally called the **Nelson's Arms** and was doubtless renamed when Nelson himself, minus one arm, visited Ludlow in 1802 to receive the Freedom of the Borough. More pubs are named after this admiral than any other person.

In an area originally of open fields, the inn had its own brewhouse at the back and stables for about half a dozen horses. There were three letting bedrooms and in 1885 the landlord was

*The **Nelson** in 2001.*

John Ingram. Seven years later an advert in the *Ludlow Advertiser* of 1892 stated that this 'well-known, fully licensed public house' was to let; 'in-going low; easy terms to a suitable tenant. Rent £18 per year'. In 1913 the licensee was Mr. D. McBride, who was still there in 1926. Better remembered though is another landlord, the late Mr. Farmer, who during a 20-year period regularly used to play dominoes. In bed at night, the present landlord frequently hears the ghostly clicking sound of dominoes being played downstairs. Nowadays a burlesque Nelson sign swings from the front of the building, replacing a more sober image of the great man, telescope to eye. However, still taking pride of place in the lounge bar is a framed copy of the classic 'The Death of Nelson at the Battle of Trafalgar' from the 1878 original wall painting by Daniel Maclise, R.A, in the Palace of Westminster.

There used to be two beerhouses nearby—the **New Inn**, which was demolished in about 1860, and the **Dun Cow**, which closed in about 1880, and is now a farmhouse.

At the next roundabout on the by-pass a minor road leads off south-eastwards towards Caynham, where a right turn takes a south-westerly course towards Ashford Carbonel. Well before reaching the village there is a crossroads with one road leading back towards Ludlow. On the west corner of the Ludlow road stands an attractive house set in pleasant gardens bearing the name the **Serpent**, which was once a public house. The original 'two-up, two down' stone cottage is believed to date from the late 16th century. It may have been just a cider house or it could have been a small inn since it lies on what used to be the main road into Ludlow from Worcester and London. Originally it was called the **Eagle and Serpent**. The local squires at Kinlet, near Cleobury Mortimer, were formerly the Childs, whose coat of arms showed an eagle and a serpent, which were meant to symbolise courage and wisdom. The inn used to be part of the nearby Ashford

*The **Serpent** at the beginning of the 21st century.*

estate and in 1781 there was a tenancy agreement, probably in relation to its being a smallholding as well. It continued as licensed premises until 1825, when the licence was not re-applied for. The property probably then became the house for the farm on the other side of the road. A new brick wing, larger and three-storeys high, was added. The present owners bought the **Serpent** as a private residence 25 years ago.

Continuing past Ashford Carbonel, the A49 is again reached and a short distance south at Woofferton is the junction with the A456 to Tenbury Wells and the B4362 to Presteigne and central Wales. Here stands the impressive looking **Salwey Arms**. It was built as a mansion house for the Salwey family in the early 19th century, before becoming an inn with a full licence in 1853. The Salweys were a prominent land-owning family with mansions in Richard's Castle and Moor Park and a house in Ludlow; over the decades six members of the family were M.Ps. for Ludlow. The family crest is a Saracen's head with the motto *Fiat voluntas Dei* (Let God's will be done).

In June 1881 the landlord was fined 40s., with costs of 16s., for selling intoxicating drink to a drunken person, and on 31 December 1894 was fined 10s, with 5s. costs, for keeping a house open for consumption of intoxicating liquor during prohibited hours. In 1885 the landlord was John Gittins, who was also a farmer. In 1891 it was advertised as 'an agricultural family and commercial hotel and posting house (John Gittens, proprietor); home comforts; charges moderate;

The Salwey Arms in 2001.

183

within 5 minutes from G.W. and L. & N.W. railway station'. In 1900 the owner was Mrs. O'Brian of Moor Park and the landlady was Elizabeth Gittins. In a licensing return of 1901 the inn was described as consisting of a kitchen, three parlours, bar and eight bedrooms with stabling for eight horses. It was owned by Lady Inchiquin, of Moor Park, and the occupier was George J. Gittins. There had been one change of ownership in the previous five years.

In 1913 George James Gittins, described also as a farmer, was landlord of the **Salwey Arms**, now called a hotel. Mrs. L. Moulton was listed as running the hotel in 1929 and again in 1941. In 1970 it was run by Mr. Harold Moulton, Shropshire's longest serving landlord. One night the hotel was broken into, Harold and his sister, Phyllis, were bound and gagged, and the robbers got away with over £200.

In the 1980s the pub became something of a centre for the youths of the area, with people travelling several miles to go to the pub on a Friday or Saturday night.

At one time the hotel had its own petrol pumps and owned the land on which the Little Chef and Travelodge now stand. The present function room was added in 1927, at first operating as a restaurant. The original stables are still in evidence.

The **Salwey Arms** was linked with the **Refreshment Rooms** at the close-by Woofferton railway station on the B4362 road to Presteigne. Today this is a derelict building at the entrance to the disused station which is now used by Orleton Building Supplies. It is

*The former **Refreshment Rooms** at Woofferton station.*

not so long ago that Woofferton was a busy junction station with the Tenbury branch of the Great Western Railway leading off the Shrewsbury and Hereford railway. Extensive timber yards adjoined the station.

The **Refreshment Rooms** held a full licence from the railway opening in 1853. According to a return of licensed houses in 1896, it was owned by Mrs. O'Brien, of

Moor Park, Ludlow, and occupied by Elizabeth Gittins, probably the wife of John Gittins, who ran the **Salwey Arms**. The **Rooms**, operating as a free house, consisted of a kitchen, parlour and refreshment room with an 'agricultural and roadside' trade. On 31 December 1894, Mrs. Gittins, just like the landlord of the **Salwey Arms**, was fined 10s., with 5s. costs, for keeping a house open for consumption of intoxicating liquor during prohibited hours. Another licensing return, of 1901, showed that the house was owned by Lady Inchiquin, of Moor Park, and the occupier was George Gittins. There was now a taproom, smokeroom and bar and its rateable value was put at £15.

The former **Rooms**, having been derelict for several years, is to be converted into a private house having been sold by the building supply firm at the turn of the millennium. On the other side of the entrance was a café, now used as an office and store. It probably stopped trading before the last war and the station finally closed to passengers in July 1961 following the closure of the Woofferton to Tenbury Wells line. Further along the B4362 is the Woofferton Transmitting Station operated by Merlin Communications International.

Another licensed property with an association with the railway is **Overton Grange**, which lies one mile south of Ludlow on the B4365. There has been a building on this site since 1066, but the present house was built in 1905 for the Betton-Foster family (motto: *nunquam non parat*—never unprepared), one of the chief landowners in Overton and Woofferton.

The two daughters were responsible for the ornate wood carvings situated on the fireplace and above the doors in the downstairs public rooms. The house later became a nursing home before taking on its present role as a privately owned small country house hotel with a restaurant, Les Marches, renowned for good food.

*The entrance to **Overton Grange**, with the locomotive number above the door.*

It is presumed that Richard Betton-Foster, an engineer, was connected with the Great Western Railway and 'orchestrated' the naming of locomotive 6879 as Overton Grange. It was the last of the Grange class to be built at Swindon Works in 1939 and cost £3,929. During the locomotive's working life, spent hauling mixed freight and occasionally passenger traffic all around the GWR region, it covered about one million miles mostly in areas where there were steep gradients. The small driving wheels of the 'Granges' made them suitable for this kind of work. The loco was withdrawn from service in 1965, sold to George Cohen and Sons as scrap, and probably ended its life in Tamworth. Today the number 6879 hangs over the vestibule door. Another curious, but totally unauthenticated story, is that a carved fireplace in one of the downstairs rooms was made from Oliver Cromwell's bedhead!

CHAPTER THIRTEEN

Clee Hill

The A4117 takes a rather tortuous route from Ludlow towards Cleobury Mortimer and eventually Bewdley and Kidderminster. Well before this it circles to the south of Titterstone Clee Hill, rising to well over 1,200 feet at Clee Hill.

The famous late 13th-century world map, the Mappa Mundi, in Hereford Cathedral, which shows the world orientated around Jerusalem, contains only one range of hills for England. These are the Clee Hills, about five miles to the east of Ludlow and a landmark for miles around. The reason for their inclusion is probably because even in those days the minerals found there were important.

For centuries the Clee Hills' industries of iron ore, lime, coal, glass, bricks and pottery continued. By 1790 some 40 coal pits were working and by the mid-19th century stone quarrying became of great importance. Up to 2,000 men, from all over Britain and Ireland, were employed in the quarries and the annual output of stone rose to over 400,000 tons. Known as dhustone, after the Celtic word for black, vast quantities were transported on the Clee Hill railway link via Bitterley to Ludlow and used for road surfaces and town and city centres throughout the country. Not unnaturally the men worked up quite a thirst in the dust and heat of the quarries and a number of public houses sprang up to cater for their needs.

The first inn on the road after the **Nelson** at Rocks Green is at Angel Bank, where once stood the **Angel Inn**. It was closed in 1992 by the then landlord who decided that it was no longer viable. The Angel sign has been in use for inns since the Middle Ages, reflecting the early connection between religious establishments and travellers' hostels. The inn started life in the 18th century as a farm with nearly 100 acres of

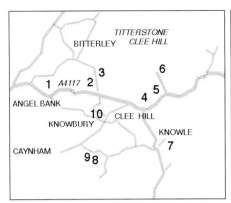

1—Angel
2—Royal Oak *
3—Dhustone
4—Golden Cross *
5—Victoria
6—Kremlin *
7—Golden Lion *
8—Bennett's End *
9—Penny Black *
10—Crown
*—*Open in 2002*

Clee Hill.

land. It is not known when it became the **Angel**, but in 1885 the licensee was given as Isaac Wheelwright. In 1913 Thomas Clent was the landlord and he was still there in 1918 when the inn and farm were put up for sale. It had been owned by the earl of Plymouth's estate who was forced to sell 3,000 acres of land in the Clee Hill area to meet tax liabilities.

A PRODUCTIVE FARM
AND A
FULLY LICENSED PUBLIC HOUSE
known as
" THE ANGEL INN,"
BITTERLEY,
extending to an area of about
97a. 2r. 36p.
THE HOUSE
is erected in Brick and Stone, and Tiled, and is situate in a prominent position to command an excellent business, and contains :—
On the Ground Floor :—Bar, Sitting Room, Club Room, Kitchen, Back Kitchen, W.C., Dairy.
On the First Floor :—4 Bedrooms.
In Basement :—Cellarage.
Outside :—Brewhouse.

THE FARM BUILDINGS
include :—Brick and tiled Piggeries. Stone and tiled Range of Hackney Stable, Granary, Mixing House, Loft, Hay Bay. Stone, timber and tiled Bull Pen, Cow Ties for 6. Stone and tiled Calves Kit, Cow Ties for 7, Calves Kit, Stable with 4 stalls, Calf House, Brick timber and iron Trap House. Stone and tiled Waggon Shed, a 4-bay Dutch Barn. Stone and tiled open Shed with enclosed Yard. Timber and iron Implement Shed. In Field No. 1017 is a Timber and iron Cattle Shed.

*Sale details for the **Angel Inn** in 1918.*

*The **Angel** from the 1918 sale catalogue.*

What happened at the sale is not clear, but in 1922 another Clent, William, was the landlord and he was still there in 1934. As well as having an extensive farm, the **Angel** was the nearest stock market to Clee and families from the village would drive their cattle there through the lanes. Often animals bolted and drovers and dogs ran for miles to bring the strays back. Pigs were even worse. The market was a social occasion.

In the early 1930s a macabre event took place at the **Angel**. Mr. Jarman, a fiddler and artist, had been married to an eastern European countess who ran off with another man. Broken hearted, he renounced all material possessions and took to the road. He had been sleeping rough in one of the out buildings when a fire occurred. The fire was eventually put out, but the charred remains of his body were found in the ashes.

Today the name lives on in 'Angel House' where the owner, who had been landlord for six

*The **Angel** in 2001.*

The Royal Oak Public House

ANGEL BANK, KNOWBURY,

together with

Enclosures of Land,

and a

COTTAGE WITH GARDEN,

The whole containing an area of about

10a. 0r. 10p.

THE HOUSE

is built of stone and tiled, and contains :—Sitting room, Tap Room, (or Kitchen) Bar, Back Kitchen, Dairy, Cellar and 3 Bedrooms.

THE OUTBUILDINGS include :—Brick stone and iron Coachhouse, Stable for 3 horses, Cowhouse with 2 ties. Two stone and tiled Piggeries.

A BRICK AND TILED COTTAGE

containing :—Kitchen, Back Kitchen, Pantry and 3 Bedrooms.

Outside :—Washhouse and Coal Store, Stable and Piggery.

SCHEDULE.

No. on Plan.	Description.	Tenant.	Area.
1006	Royal Oak Inn, Building, Cottage and Gardens ..	Ind Coope & Co., Ltd.	.455
1003	Pasture	do. ..	.183
716	do.	do. ..	1.041
996	do.	do.	3.531
394	do.	do.	.923
395	do.	do.	.092
1005	do.	do.	.289
1004	do.	do.	.260
1002	do.	do.	.412
1001	do.	do.	·459
1000	do.	do.	.364
995	do.	do.	1.194
1007	do.	do.	.864
		Total ..	10.067

This Lot is leased for a term of 14 years from Ladyday 1912.

*Details and photograph of the **Royal Oak** from the 1918 sale catalogue.*

190

*The **Royal Oak** sign..*

*The 1932 **Royal Oak** tug-of-war team.*

years, still lives and also provides *en-suite* self-catering accommodation in the Cottage, part of the main building, and the Bakehouse Studio, the former bakehouse barn.

Further along the road, on the same side, is the **Royal Oak**, believed to date in part from the 18th century and expanded in the mid-

*The **Royal Oak** in 2001.*

19th century to cater for the increased quarrying trade. John Watkins was the landlord in 1913. Then in 1918, like the **Angel Inn**, it was put up for sale by the earl of Plymouth and sold for £1,250.

Ernest Martin was landlord in the 1920s, while Frederick Stubbs was in charge in 1941. His wife maintained that the parish boundary line, between Bitterley and Caynham, ran through the pub.

In January 2002 the **Royal Oak** was put up for sale again, based on an asking price of about £200,000. The inn was described as containing a main lounge, snug, bar, games room, large function room, and three bedrooms. The games room is where the dairy was located, an area later used as a sweet shop and then as a fish and chip shop. A slaughterhouse and butcher's used to be where the toilets are now. Underneath the building is a natural spring.

Climbing Clee Hill one comes to the village of Clee, described as 'bleak, barren and inaccesible' and not marked on a map until 1885.

*Customers outside the **Dhustone Inn** in 1939.*

Down Dhustone Lane was the **Dhustone Inn**, one of many pubs catering for the needs of thirsty workers employed in quarrying. In the 1860s Clee Hill experienced its own industrial revolution when there were up to 2,000 workers imported from various parts of Britain employed in the stone quarries, coal mines and on the railway. There was even a Clee Hill dialect, which everyone spoke until the Second World War (including 'muthers' - bottoms of a barrel of beer; 'ok shut' - hog's head barrel; 'sup' - to drink; and 'a lat chaver' - enough for a pint).

The **Dhustone Inn**, which was named after the local black rock that was quarried and used in road building, was built in the late 19th century, primarily for the quarrymen. It was run by William Walter in the 1910s and '20s and Walter Roberts who was there in 1923. The Roberts family, apparently, had very dark eyebrows, giving rise to the pub's nickname, 'The Darkies'. It was then taken over by Alfred Richard (Dick) Jenkins in the 1930s. While his wife, Marjorie, ran the pub, which sold cider and beer only, Jenkins was the village undertaker, wheelwright, small-holder and also cultivated a

Customers with a whisket.

large garden. This was the birthplace of Alf Jenkins, who became a teacher and wrote *Titterstone Clee Hills* in which he describes in vivid detail what life in a pub was then like:

> The quarrying of stone was a very dusty, thirsty process and there was little or no time allowed to walk to the pub during working hours. Therefore boys were employed to carry cider to the men. These boys had earthenware jars which usually had 'whiskets' [wicker baskets] to protect them. If a 'whisket' was not used the jars were frequently broken accidentally by catching them on jagged rocks ... As each lunch-time approached my mother drew twenty or thirty pints of cider and placed them on trays. As the door bolt was drawn back the quarrymen rushed into the public bar and sat down. The trays of cider were taken to them and the money collected afterwards.
>
> The furnishings of the public house were bare and rough because the workmen's clothes were always covered with dust and tar. After each lunch hour, it was necessary to wash all the seats and tables to ensure protection of the clothes of evening customers.
>
> Beneath the wooden seats there were piles of cast iron spittoons. These were partially filled with sawdust and in constant use. Although a disgusting habit, I often admired the accuracy with which these men could spit great distances.

Alf recalled that draught cider cost 4d. a pint, beer was 1s. 2d. and porter 1s. 6d. Sometimes arguments, usually about football or impending elections, erupted and his mother defused the situation by blowing a whistle and shouting 'Half-time'.

'Saturday night was always a jolly time', he continued. 'Every person seemed to have his own party piece to offer. The usual procedure was for one person to sing a song, recite a poem, tell a joke or play an instrument. When he had finished everyone else was encouraged to emulate him with the instruction, "Sing, say, or pay"'.

'At weddings', he continued, 'the guests had a peculiar custom of bringing two or three new glazed chamberpots to the public house which were filled up with beer and ceremoniously handed around all the customers to have a drink', and 'when a family came to see dad to do the undertaking he was invariably asked to take a case or two of beer when delivering the coffin'. The Jenkins family left the inn in 1962. At some point it was given a false black and white exterior and in the 1970s it was famous for its beer-drinking pony.

The quarry industry continues today with one of the three quarries still open, but the railway line from Ludlow to Bitterley closed many years ago and the **Dhustone Inn** closed down in the early 1980s. It was bought as a private house in 1984 and is now called Rowan House.

*The **Dhustone** closed in the 1980s and is now a private house.*

In the High Street of Clee village is the **Golden Cross**. It is not clear why the cross became golden and many early cross tavern signs were changed because of Puritan disapproval. But this particular **Cross** was probably only built in the 19th century. The first reference to the **Golden Cross** seems to be in 1884 when an auction was held that year at the inn for the sale of 'valuable freehold property and building sites'. The first lot was for 'a piece of Valuable Freehold Land containing 1,980 square yards freehold land, situate near the Golden Cross Inn, adjoining the road leading to Tenbury, and having a frontage thereto of 90ft'. Another six lots of land were also for sale. Lot 7 was 'a dwelling house with out-buildings and very productive garden, while Lot 8 was a valuable field. Lots 1,2,3,4 and 5 are all valuable sites for building purposes and command extensive views. Each plot has a right of Common thereon'.

A copy of the sale poster, found in the attic by a previous landlord, hangs on the wall of the public bar. Also displayed is an old photograph, dated

*The **Golden Cross** in 2001.*

1901, showing shops across the road, including Jenners Central Stores which burnt down in 1935 and was replaced by a private residence.

In 1885 William Bate was landlord of the **Golden Cross**. An inventory and valuation was carried out on 13 May 1902 by Edward Key for Thomas Blytheway involving four hogshead casks valued at £2. The inn was described as having a bar, back bar, front room, back room, and kitchen.

By the side of the pub, Goods Shed Lane led past nearby houses built up the hillside where, by the side of the railway, once stood a large store built to house delivered provisions. Henry Bate was landlord of the **Golden Cross** in 1913 and is also mentioned in 1926. In 1941 the licensee was Leonard Green.

At the end of the village on the corner of the High Street is a block of flats, which once housed the **Victoria Inn**, named presumably after Queen Victoria. The first record of the inn is in 1877 when William Hatton, described as a shopkeeper, took out a mortgage on the **Victoria** for £100 with Joseph Swift, of Burford, gentleman. Hatton recites the will (25 Feb 1874) and codicil (13 Apr 1874) of Richard Hatton, of Clee Hill. In consideration of £100 and interest, are mentioned 320 square yards in the **Victoria Inn** garden (with recently erected messuages), the well and land called

Serious looking customers outside the ***Victoria*** *in 1930.*

*The **Victoria** has been turned into flats.*

Far Meadow, Cainham, with insurance policy. George Lynall was the innkeeper for some years before moving in 1892 to the nearby **Golden Lion Inn**, where he died a year later. In 1913 the landlord was Benjamin Martin and in 1941 it was Frederick Slater. The inn closed about 1960.

Going north along the lane by the **Victoria**, you eventually come to the curiously named **Kremlin Inn**. Is it a Russian outpost, one wonders, a corruption of a previous name or just a landlord's whim? It was, apparently, the old quarry master's house before becoming an inn. Originally it was called the **Craven Arms**, being named after the earl of Craven, the absentee landlord at Stokesay Castle who was a major landholder in the area. From at least 1913 to 1926 the inn was run by Mrs. Mary Hammond and in 1934 the landlady was Olicey Poole. In 1941 the landlord was William Gittings.

During the 1950s and '60s, when the Cold War between the West and the Soviet Union was at its height, quarrels and the odd fracas would break out in the inn. This led to its taking up the nickname of **Kremlin**, or **Krem**. Another theory is that the inn began to pick up Radio Moscow on its radio and television. The interference could have come from the radar station, used by the Civil Aviation Authority, on top of

*The **Kremlin** at the beginning of the 21st century.* Titterstone Clee or

Extracted by *Clark & co Solicitors, Ludlow.*

In Her Majesty's High Court of Justice.

BE IT KNOWN, that at the date hereunder written, the last Will and Testament . . . . (a Copy whereof is hereunto annexed) of

George Lynall
of The Golden Lion Inn, Knowle, Clee Hill in the County of Salop, Innkeeper, formerly of The Victoria Inn, Clee Hill aforesaid

deceased, who died on the *13th* day of *December* 18*93* at *the Knowle aforesaid*

who at the time of *his* death had a fixed place of abode at *the Knowle aforesaid* , within the District of *the Counties of Salop and Montgomery*

was proved and registered in the District Probate Registry of Her Majesty's High Court of Justice, at *Shrewsbury*
and that Administration of the personal estate of the said deceased was granted by the aforesaid Court to

Sarah Anne Lynall
Widow the Relict of the said deceased the Sole Executrix

named in the said *Will she* . . . . . having been first sworn well and faithfully to administer the same.

And it is hereby certified that an Affidavit in verification of the Account of the said estate has been delivered duly stamped wherein it is shown that the gross value of the said estate amounts to £ *372* . *14* . *9* . and no more.

Dated the *3rd* day of *February* 18*94*

Fred. R. Walton
District Registrar

*Probate of the will of George Lynall of the **Golden Lion**, who died on 13 December 1893.*

even from Woofferton Transmitting station. Going east, there is no ground as high till the Urals are reached.

Whatever the reason, the then landlord decided to change the name and in about 1986 the **Kremlin** sign went up. Recently the pub was visited by Russian tourists. 'Now we have been to two Kremlins' they told the landlord, and left the name written on his business card in the Cyrillic alphabet.

Leaving Clee Hill by the B4214 towards Tenbury Wells leads first to the village of Knowle where, down the appropriately named Lion Lane, is the **Golden Lion**. The

*Events at the **Golden Lion** in the 1920s.*

current landlord has numerous deeds, mortgages and other documents on the property in his possession which make fascinating reading. Originally two cottages called Stokes, it was built of local sandstone in the early 19th century

198

after the site had been enclosed from common land. William Wilden lived there until he died in 1837 when he left it to his son, George. In 1849 George, a shoe-maker, sold it to Mr. William Page, innkeeper, for £90.

*The **Golden Lion** at the beginning of the 21st century.*

Stokes was bought for £400 in 1868 by Joshua Hammonds, of Corely, collier and miner, from William Smith, farmer. At the same time he took out a mortgage for £250 on the property, now in the occupation of Thomas Hammonds. In 1877 there was a marriage at St. Mary's Church, Burford, between William Birch, 50, widower, a farmer of Stoddeston, and Elizabeth Hammonds, 55, widow, innkeeper of the **Knowle**. Her father William Pope was also an innkeeper. In 1892 George Lynall, who ran the **Victoria Inn**, Clee Hill, took over the **Golden Lion Inn**. Inside a year, he was dead and left the property to his widow, Sarah Ann.

In 1922 Sarah Lynnall died leaving the **Lion Inn** to Thomas Edwin Vale, a pawnbroker's assistant from Walsall, and £200 to Mr. John Nelson Pitt, 'of the Lion Inn'. 'Jack' Pitt was also the village undertaker and wheelwright and one of the first persons in the area to own a motor car. In 1946 Thomas Vale sold the **Golden Lion Inn** to Pitt for £900. In 1947 Pitt in turn sold the inn and 3/4 acre to Wilfred Bowen, grocer, of Cradley, Worcester and his wife Florence for £5,000. In 1958, the **Golden Lion** was owned by Frederick Smith Ltd., who sold it to W. Butler and Co. Ltd.

In 1970 it was sold by Mitchells and Butlers to Bass Holdings for the repeat figure of £5,000, from whom Charles Whiteman bought it in 1985 for £22,000. It was about that time that a brick extension, of dubious aesthetic quality, was added to more than double the size of the original stone building. The inn was sold again in 1995 for £83,000. It is now the headquarters of the Clee Hill Rugby Club, founded in 1998.

Bennett's End in 2002. The inn sign sports a weathervane.

It is not often that you come across two large public houses side by side in the middle of nowhere, but that is what is found in the village of Knowbury, with **Bennett's End** and the **Penny Black**, whose past is inextricably linked. To begin with there was just the former inn, probably built in 1640, or so the sign says. It stood on an even older site; underneath the building is a water catchment believed to date from Roman times and connecting with Oak Court in Bagot when it was part of that estate. At any rate, it was an old coaching inn, built of local stone with large stables, being at one time on the main road from Ludlow and Snitton through to Hope Bagot and Tenbury. It also had an old brewing licence. Legend has it that the inn was called **Bennett's End** after a man called Bennett, possibly a naval captain, who hanged

*The **Penny Black** in 2002.*

200

himself nearby. However, a more prosaic reason is that a former landlord, who was also a farmer, had the name Thomas Bennetts Clent. This was in 1885. Certainly it was known at one time simply as the **End Inn**.

Towards the latter part of the 19th century the inn's trade found fresh impetus with the building of an aqueduct, taking water from Rhayader in Wales to Birmingham, across two streams and a marshy valley at the bottom of its garden. Thomas Matthews was landlord in 1913 and was still there in 1926, but by 1941 Wilfred Brothers was running **End Inn**. In the 1950s and 60s it was owned by Mr. Trace, who was also a dentist, and his wife, parents of Christopher Trace of Blue Peter fame. Then between 1961 and 1984 it was run as a family affair with Sid Massey, also a builder, his wife, parents, and sister, Belinda, and four children. Belinda was married to Ashley Paston-Cooper, an airline pilot in Bahrain.

The stables were demolished in the early 1960s to make way for a car park and, as the family grew and trade increased, with many customers from the Black Country, Sid Massey built an extension from local old timbers. Originally it was to have been called the **Dreaded End** but then, in 1972, it became the **Bitter End** as it grew to be a pub in its own right. The new owner, Brian Cook, changed the name to **Penny Black** (named after the first adhesive postage stamp, issued in 1840) when he took over in 1984, with the two houses being sold separately. Rumour has it that the inn was built following a family dispute but this appears to be unfounded.

To add to legend and rumour, there is now a ghost. According to the present licensees, it appears wearing a long black army trench coat. It opens all the fridges day and night, a vacuum cleaner drones at four in the morning, a heavy fire door opens, and beer mats litter the floor. Then there is the chill factor, like ice in the

*A torn photograph of the **Crown** in 1910.*

201

SOUTH SHROPSHIRE.
CLEE HILL.

⬚⬚⬚

PARTICULARS of an IMPORTANT FREEHOLD FULLY-LICENSED PROPERTY,

with possession on completion of purchase.

⬚⬚⬚

The FREE HOUSE, known as the

Crown Inn, Knowbury

situate near the main CAINHAM-CLEE HILL ROAD, four-and-a-half miles from the TOWN OF LUDLOW.

THE PROPERTY, principally constructed of brick with tiled roof, contains the following:

INTERIOR ACCOMMODATION—

> Basement: Two Dry Cellars.
> Ground Floor: Bar, Bar Parlour, Snug, Smoke Room—21ft. × 16ft., Club Room—40ft. × 18ft., Serving Room, Office, Spirit Store Room, Large Living Kitchen, Back Kitchen, Dairy, Spacious Brew House, well equipped with a modern plant.
> First Floor: Five Bed Rooms and a Landing.

OUTSIDE—Wood and Coal Stores.   GARDEN.

THE RANGE OF BUILDINGS

include STABLING for 11, with lofts, COW HOUSE, with ties for 3, CALVES' COTE, GRANARY, and 2 PIGGERIES.

THE LAND,

in a ring fence, is OLD PASTURE, divided into convenient well-watered enclosures in good heart, having for many years been exceedingly well treated, the whole being of an area of about

18 acres,   2 roods,   39 perches,

*Sale of the **Crown** in 1920.*

pool room where it should be warm. Both pubs are now owned by Mr. W.J. Twitchell, of Whitton Court.

Not far away in the village of Knowbury is Crown House which used to be another well-known coaching inn, the **Crown**. The inn is mentioned in the 1781 census, but it could well date back to 1710. A licence was issued to John Bowen in 1783, at a time when licences to sell alcoholic liquor were first issued throughout the country, and other licences were granted to Timothy Howat in 1810 and Ann Harvatt in 1822. In 1827 the inn included some 56 acres of ground.

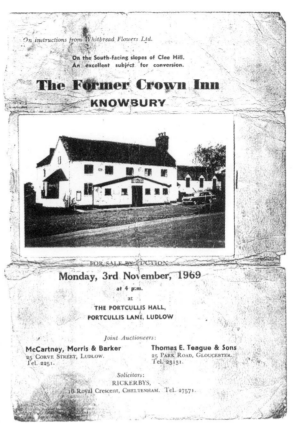

A battered copy of the 1969 sale particulars.

By 1854 another Bowen had taken over the licence and the census of 1881 shows that the innkeeper was John Bowen, aged 35, who lived there with his wife, Elizabeth, aged 34, four children, a servant and her son, and a groom. There was a nearby toll-gate and on the corner of Scott's Lane opposite is London House, where pilgrims used to stay.

John Bowen was still the landlord in 1910, but in 1920 the inn was put up for sale by auction at the **Feathers Hotel** in Ludlow by Elizabeth Bowen, who then held the licence. The property comprised two dry cellars, a bar, bar parlour, snug, smoke room, large club room, serving room, office, spirit store room, large living kitchen, back kitchen, dairy, a spacious brew house well equipped with a modern plant, and five bedrooms. The **Crown** was purchased by Mrs. Sarah

Wheelwright, who was still there in 1926. John Rewbury was the landlord in 1941.

Later, the **Crown** became a 'lively' place, with dances and discos held in a building extension. 'Rowdy' was another adjective sometimes used. After a rumpus one night in 1968, the police were called, fisticuffs ensued and the landlord lost his licence. After standing empty for a while the inn was sold in 1971, mainly for the land, and is now a private house. The extension was knocked down and replaced with two houses.

'That Ale's the true liquor of life'

(*Praise of Ale*, a 17th century ballad).

Postscript

It may appear from the preceding pages that in the past Ludlow has suffered, if that is the right word, from a surfeit of inns and alehouses and that every other house was selling some kind of liquid refreshment. In this you would be wrong, and yet there are a great many more named establishments which do not appear simply because it is not known where they were situated. Then there are the more humble beer-houses which never had a name and have literally disappeared into the mists of time. Set against this seeming plethora of places in which to imbibe, it is more than likely that some of the names referred to the same building at different times in its life.

The chief source for these otherwise unknown, but named pubs is Edmund Jones in his book *Old Inns of Ludlow*, dated 1913, in which were listed in the following chronological order:

Hunting Horse, Queen Anne's Head, Serjeant (1742)
Running Horse, King David (1743)
Shears, Shoe & Boot (1747)
Hand & Shears (1748)
Ring of Bells, Mare and Groom, Mason's Arms (1749)
Holly Bush, Guns (1756)
Pistols (1757)
Guns and Pistols, Horn, Coffee House (1758)
Jolly Gardener (1759)
Golden Fleece, Golden Heart (1760)
Shoulder of Mutton (1764)
Tap House (1769)
Duke's Arms (1791)
Black Horse (1793).

In addition, Harry Baker, in his *Alphabet of Ludlow Pubs*, dated 1983, mentions the **Rose and the Three Cups** in the Bull Ring and a **White Bear** near the **Unicorn** in Corve Street.

Bibliography

In the following lists the sources are given in date of publication order where appropriate.

GENERAL WORKS
English Social History, G.M. Trevelyan, 1944
Buildings of England series - Shropshire, N. Pevsner, 1958
The King's England - Shropshire, A. Mee, 1968

THE COUNTY
Nooks & Corners of Shropshire, H.T. Timmins, 1899
Shropshire, E. Vale, 1949
Shropshire, M. Herring, 1949
Portrait of Shropshire, B. Bailey, 1981
Shropshire Folklore, edited by C. Burns, 1882
Titterstone Clee Hills, A.E. Jenkins, 1983
Shropshire Curiosities, G. Glover, 1989
Shropshire: A History, B. Trinder, 1998
Shropshire Towns and Villages, J. Meech, 2000
South Shropshire in Old Photographs, D. Trumper, 2001
A History of Stanton Lacy Parish, C. Smout

THE TOWN
The History & Antiquities of Ludlow, T. Wright, 1822
Broad Street, D.J. Lloyd, 1979
A Ludlow Album, Bill Webb, 1981
Ludlow in Old Picture Postcards, M. Speight, 1983
Ludlow: A Historic Town in Words and Pictures, D.J. Lloyd & P. Klein, 1984
The Feathers, D.J. Lloyd, P. Howell, M. Richards, 1986
The Misericords & Choir Stalls of Ludlow Parish Church, P. Klein, 1986
Ludlow 1085-1660: A Social, Economic and Political History, M.A. Faraday, 1991
The Buildings of Ludlow, R. Morriss & K. Hoverd, 1993
The Concise History of Ludlow, D. Lloyd, 1999

JOURNALS AND NEWSPAPERS ETC.

Kelly's Directories of Herefordshire, various years
Kelly's Dirctories of Shropshire, various years
Universal British Directory
Pigot's London & Provincial Directory
Shropshire Gazeteer
Robson's Directory of Salop
Slater's Directory of Shropshire
Bagshaw Gazeteer of Shropshire
Porter's Directory of Salop
Ludlow Heritage News, Ludlow Civic Society
A New Guide to the Town of Ludlow, 1822
Ludlow, Chamber of Trade & Commerce Official Guide, 1992
Footsteps Down Mill Street, G. Merchant
Shropshire Legends & People, Shropshire Publications
Ludlow Advertiser
Shropshire Magazine
Shropshire Star
Diaries, T. Griffiths, Ludlow printer, 1826-1829
Day Book, T. Griffiths, 1816-1826 and 1840-1844

INNS AND TAVERNS

Inns, Ales And Drinking Customs of Old England, F.W. Hackwood, 1909
The Old Inns of England, A.E. Richardson, 1934
Pub Names of Britain, L. Dunkling and G. Wright, 1994
The Pubs of Hereford City, R. Shoesmith, 1998
The Pubs of Leominster, Kington & north-west Herefordshire,
      R. Shoesmith & R. Barrett, 2000.
Beer and Britannia, Peter Haydon, 2001

Index of Pub Names

In the following index common names are used—others are cross-referenced. Adjectival descriptions are normally used except for 'new' and 'old'. To avoid confusion the parish or village is shown for country inns; in Ludlow the street is shown. Only the main entries are indexed.

Imperial Vaults (White Lion, Bear & White Lion, Prince Rupert) (Old Street)   119-22

Keysell's (Wine Vaults) (Bull Ring)   87
King's Arms (Ye Old King's Arms) (Bull Ring)   102-4
Kremlin Inn (Craven Arms) (Clee Hill)   196-8

Lamb (Holy Lamb) (Corve Street)   154
Lion Inn (Golden Lion) (Knowle)   199
Lower Fox (Birmingham Arms) (Upper Galdeford)   166
Ludlow Arms (Whitcliffe, Bowling Green) (Whitcliffe)   173-5
Ludlow Castle (Castle Inn) (Castle)   21-2

Mare & Groom (Horse & Jockey) (Old Street)   131
Mermaid (Lower Broad Street)   76
Mr Underhill's at Dinham Weir (Dinham)   27
Mitre (Corve Street)   146-7
Mitre (Half Moon) (Lower Galdford)   172
Mortimer's Castle (Mortimer's Tower, Mug House) (Castle)   22-4
Mortimer's Tower (Mortimer's Castle) (Castle)   20
Mug House (Mortimer's Castle) (Castle)   24
Mug House (Old Gate, Drum, Dog, Tap House, Friars Inn) (Old Street)   128-30

Nag's Head (Corve Street)   149-51
Nag's Head (Paul Pry) (Lower Broad Street)   74
Nelson Inn (Nelson's Arms) (Rocks Green)   181
Nelson's Arms (Nelson Inn) (Rocks Green)   181
New Crown (Red Lion) (Market Street)   110
New Fox (Birmingham Arms) (Upper Galdeford)   166
New Inn (New Road)   166
New Inn (Rocks Green)   182
New Inn (Stanton Lacy)   179
New Inn (Upper Galdeford)   167-8
New Wine Cellars (Wine Vaults) (Bull Ring)   86

Old Fox (Birmingham Arms) (Upper Galdeford)   166
Old Gate (Mug House) (Old Street)   128
Old Red Lion (Red Lion) (Market Street)   110-2
Old Running Horse (Trotting Horse) (Corve Street)   149
Old Stag's Head (Robert Dul's tavern) (Lower Broad Street)   77
Overton Grange (Overton)   185

Paul Pry (Nag's Head) (Lower Broad Street)   74
Peacock (Broad Street)   61
Penny Black (Dreaded End, Bitter End) (Knowbury)   200-1
Pheasant Inn (Old Street)   126
Plough (Raven Lane)   115-6
Plumbers Arms (Borough Arms) (Raven Lane)   113
Plume of Feathers (Raven Lane)   117
Pound & Patch (Upper Hayton)   181
Portcullis (Upper Galdeford)   163-4
Portcullis (Blue Boar) (Mill Street)   29
Prince of Wales (White Horse) (Raven Lane)   117
Prince Rupert (Imperial Vaults) (Old Street)   119-21

Queen's (Queen's Head) (Lower Galdeford)   170-1
Queen's Arms (Bridge Inn) (Corve Street)   144-6
Queen's Head (Queen's) (Lower Galdeford)   169-71

Raven (Gravel Hill)   165
Raven (Raven Lane)   112-3
Rayndeer (Talbot) (Broad Street)   67
Red Lion (Globe Inn) (Market Street)   108
Red Lion (New Crown, Old Red Lion) (Market Street)   110-2
Refreshment Rooms (Woofferton)   183-4
Robert Dul's tavern (Old Stag's Head) (Lower Broad Street)   77
Red Lion (Falcon) (Old Street)   127
Rose & Crown (Church Street)   45-7
Rose & Crown (Corve Street)   154